Molly Seymour is a young writer who got into writing because he wanted to find a creative way to inspire people, to get people talking about what he feels is an injustice in our society particularly when it comes to disabled people. There is a loss off human potential as disabled people, a part of human evolution, are constantly ignored. Now even though disabilities aren't seen as the ideal body type but behind their disability, the people are just the same as any one of us. We all have a desire to be loved, we all have a desire to be happy and we all certainly have a desire to be successful, no matter our background. By helping disabled people, Molly is helping humanity move forward to becoming a more accepting society and you can help him by supporting this book. Doing so, you are playing your part in humanity embracing humanity as a whole. Thankyou.

William John Little, Sigmund Freud, William Osler, Dr Pierre Maroteaux, Jean Lobstein, Wilem Vrolik, David Silence, Jean Martin Charcot, Karl Landsteiner, Erwin Popper, Dr Robert Whytt, Sir Charles Bell, John Hughlings Jackson, Dr Dorothy Hansine Anderson, Dr Paul Di Saint Agnese, Rudolf Ludwig Virchow, Dr James Morton, Guilame Benjamin Duchenne, George's Giles de la Tourette, John Bulwer, Thomas Braidwood, Thomas Gallaudet, Alice Cogswell, Louis Braille, Edward Rushton, George Huntington, Fred Plum, Wilhelm Conrad Roentgen, James Parkinson, John Langdon Down, Professor Jerômé Lejeune.

Molly Seymour

A BRIEF HISTORY OF DISABILITY

AUSTIN MACAULEY PUBLISHERS™

LONDON * CAMBRIDGE * NEW YORK * SHARJAH

The medical information in this book is not advice and should not be treated as such. Do not substitute this information for the medical advice of physicians. The information is general and intended to better inform readers of their health care. Always consult your doctor for your individual needs.

A CIP catalogue record for this title is available from the British Library.

ISBN 9781035826674 (Paperback)
ISBN 9781035826681 (Hardback)
ISBN 9781035826704 (ePub e-book)
ISBN 9781035826698 (Audiobook)

www.austinmacauley.com

First Published 2023
Austin Macauley Publishers Ltd®
1 Canada Square
Canary Wharf
London
E14 5AA

The reason why I wanted to write this book was to help disabled people. I wanted to stop the stigma that they feel daily, to make them feel included in society. It also happens to be a hidden part of human history which isn't talked about. In order to truly understand disability, I knew I had to start from the beginning through its history. There's a quote from Rod Laver which still means a lot to me, *in order to find the true understanding of something, you've got to learn about its history and see how it has evolved over time.* Which exactly what this book sets out to do. This book is here to teach the world that disabled people are the same as able-bodied people. They have the same feelings, dreams and ambitions in life as we do but because they look different, they are misrepresented. When I can prove that our mind is what defines us not our bodies, I really hope you take this newfound information, help disabled people, don't ignore them; it's not their fault they have the bodies they have—it's genetics. Thank you so much for reading it.

Molly Seymour

Table of Contents

Introduction

Throughout all our lives, we all know someone that is considered disabled or if you haven't then, we've at least seen them on TV, whether they are wheelchair bound because of lack of mobility, are speech impaired, blind or deaf. But very few know about the origins of disability as in recent times, it is considered a taboo in our society, which I do wonder why as disabled people have been around even longer than records began. I guess it comes down to the idea of a perfect human society where everyone that is born human should have a perfectly working body to be a part of a perfect society. The reality is far complex than this as there is no such thing as a perfect society.

I'll explain that disability is governed by two major factors, the first one is biology and the second is our environment. This book will show you that disabled people have played a huge part in our human evolution; it has certainly changed our perception of being human that there isn't just one body but there are many bodies to be human, all with their unique parts. I hope to inspire a generation of people that will embrace disability and not to be scared or dismiss them and learn that disability isn't a barrier to anyone and disability certainly doesn't define us. Society has taught us to not talk to disabled people when they are only the same as able bodied. By changing the term disability to different ability, our mindsets towards disabled people can be changed. We all just need to open our minds and learn so we can create a better understanding between able-bodied people and disabled people so that they can have rights too.

I'm Molly Seymour and throughout my life, I have always been curious to find out more about disabled people why they are the way they are, and why do they exist? I promise in an innocent and caring way, I have been asking the same questions almost my entire life and luckily for us, I have the answers. Come with me as I explore a hidden human history that rarely gets talked about. I have chosen 20 different disabilities that are well known in our society such as Cerebral Palsy, Brittle Bones, Paralysis, Spina Bifida and Dwarfism, to only name a few as I'll be explaining:

What these disabilities are?
The story of their unique history.
Who were the people who first discovered them?
Finding out the genetics that cause them.
How these disabilities are today?

This is a brief history of disability.

Chapter I
A Hidden History of Disability

The Beginning of Disability

If you asked me, how far back does disability go, well, I can safely say since the start of humanity. Legend has it that disabled people have always been around but the earliest recorded signs of the disabled dates back to the dawn of cave men and women, where it was a story of survival of the fittest, not just for our bodies but for our genetics. As disability is caused by two main components-nutrition and the environment. Nutrition is a major factor because we need nutrients to help keep the cells in our bodies healthy. Without it, our bodies just simply can't keep going; so over time, our bodies will eventually stop working and deteriorate, what we call disability, One of the oldest disabilities known to man is a condition called osteogenesis imperfecta (brittle bones disease). Around 250,000 years ago, an ice age swept the whole of Europe and our early ancestors were there to see it; the ice age was the cause of brittle bones because Europe was so cold that the cold air, snow and thick clouds blocked the sun's rays. We know that the sun is full of vitamin D essential for healthy bones and played a huge role in human evolution, that's just to name an example. So, let's go back in time millions and millions of years ago, even before modern humans came around.

Cave Men and Women

We're going to go back in time, back to when cave men and women were around. It's no secret that evolution has been happening for millions of years and with it comes disability. Evolution is carried out with one main law which is natural selection, which is where we our genes from both our mothers and fathers; this is where genes mutate even before we are born. Genetic mutation is the cause of a disability.

At the moment, chimpanzees are the closet relative we have living on earth with us. Evolution has created different species of human. Such as homo habilis, homo errectus (tall man), homo heidelbergensis, homo rhodesiensis and homo sapiens, to only name a few of course. When homo habilis was around roughly 2.5 million years ago, this time period would've been just before the time that natural selection occurred, as homo habilis and homo errectus breeded with each other which created more species of human such as homo heidelbergensis and homo rhodesiensis. When they interbred together, this was when homo sapiens were born, which would make sense as homo sapiens are the most advanced humans that have ever walked the planet. Our genetics have been really kind to us by allowing us to have the best traits of homo heidelbergensis and rhodesiensis. These two humans before us allowed us to become the most advanced humans ever. Our unique and advanced brain with the ability to communicate with other humans, and to have imagination to plan and learn how the world works has proved vital for our survival. The most amazing thing which I've discovered is that homo sapiens did interbreed with homo Neanderthals, which was a human species based in Europe. They were the first settlers of human to make it to France and England. What was incredible was our genetics seemed to be more advanced than theirs because not many genetics for the Neanderthals exist today; the majority of our genes today are from our homo sapiens ancestors.

You would think that if homo sapiens bred with homo Neanderthals, our genes would be shared equally, but no, our genetics seem to be far superior which is one of the reasons why the Neanderthals became extinct because we were far more advanced for them to keep up. So, what does this have to do with disability? Well, at this time, genetic mutations might have started when homo sapiens interbred with the Neanderthals as some genes were similar as both species were human and some genes were unique. As we know based on the Egyptians that too many genes that are similar cause our genes to mutate and cause birth defects and disabilities before birth. So, this is why disability has been around even when we were cave men and women.

Disability was around but so little is known about this time period. We know that it is not just interbreeding that is the only cause of disability; other causes are there as well, such as nutrition and the environment. Our ever-changing climate has been the cause of human disability for hundreds and thousands of years. Dwarfism has been a result of this.

During the incredible human journey, some homo sapiens travelled to India, then Europe while other homo sapiens travelled south east to the Flores Islands which is in Indonesia. It was very hard to find the right nutrients such as minerals and vitamins to stabilise the body cells. Humidity drained the bodies of homo sapiens so much that it caused their bodies to evolve to shrink to only being 3ft tall. These species of human were called homo floresiensis. They were only 3ft tall but they had advanced brains to survive and adapt to their environment. Scientists are in debate on whether homo sapiens interbred with floresiensis as there is very little evidence to support this theory but if they didn't, then how does it explain that there are people living with dwarfism today? There's got be genes from homo floresiensis which is the cause of dwarfism today.

Of course, there is another theory that an ice age that swept the whole of Europe that caused ever-changing damage to the bodies of homo sapiens such as skeletal dysplasia, which is linked with the condition achondroplasia-the most common form of dwarfism. So, we now have an idea of where disability started and still is prevalent today.

So, this is just an idea of how long disabled people have lived with us, so what about its cause? Well, before I wrote this book, I started getting ideas myself which developed me into developing a theory of my own.

My Theory

My theory takes us back to time where there was more than one species of humans; to when homo sapiens ruled our planet for hundreds and thousands of years. It starts with the basic from of biology. We all know that men have sperm cells and women have egg cells, but the tiny cells inside these cells is what makes biology so magical. When the sperm cell meets the egg cells, it multiplies, which we know, but what we don't know yet is that there are extra group of cells that are deeply hidden within the sperm and the egg cells these are called X-cells (unknown cells); you could call this the Big Bang of cells because as soon as the sperm cells fertilise the egg, an explosion of cells erupts producing the ingredients that make a human body. These cells are highly complex and individual in their own unique way which makes us so unique as well. These cells are both good and unfortunately bad; good cells are healthy cells which are supported by nutrients and minerals to stay stable while our babies grow and develop. We also have bad cells which are made from lack of nutrition or extreme environmental causes. These cells play an important role in the growing process. Why don't we come up with a name for them? Let's call them X-cells; you'll find that they can be good but also bad, good as they help protect the good genes, a bit like how cytotoxic T cells, which help destroy the bad X-cells, but only up to a point. The bad X-cells are caused by lack of nutrition and nutrients, and minerals to support them, so they attack the healthy ones to gain stability for themselves. The bad X-cells are stronger and they can break down good cells when the body's defences are too weak to tackle them and so bad X-cells that can destroy the good ones. These X-cells are tinier than we can see through a telescope after the fertilisation of an egg. Another way of putting it is, let's say, the good X-cells are blue and the bad X-cells are red, for example. Both the man and the woman X-cells combine and they fight the stronger cells; the blue X-cells are there to sort out the genetics of what the baby will inherit from the mum and dad whereas the red X-cells sadly destroy the blue X-cells. In the process, the mutated cells carry on and evolve with the good X-cells; it's important to point out that once a gene is mutated, nothing can cure it; not even evolution.

These X-cells continue to fight until the right amount of X-cells are there to expand the larger cells; that's where they multiply. Our genes are made up of A, C, G, T genes which are the proteins that make the human body. The X-cells have done their job if 1 letter out of the A, C, G, T changes; so, if you have A, C, H, T, that is the result of a gene mutation. Once the damage is done, the genes grow with the mutation as the baby grows in the womb. This gives our bodies the birth defects we know today. The environment also plays a vital role on X-cells because even though you've eaten properly, the extreme weather conditions can affect the X-cells in the same way it damages them which leads the genes to mutate. So, disability has been around a lot longer than anyone could ever imagine. So, at a time living as cave men and women, it would've been hard to get all the nutrients and minerals required for a healthy body. And ever-changing climates would've also had ever-changing effects on our bodies forever. As we know our genes travel down our family tree for centuries, so would disability too.

Disability in Ancient Times

In the ancient times, if you had a disability, people in the community saw you as to have a curse or it was a condition that you got from God. In 470–399 BC, great philosophers who lived around this time taught the able-bodied people to not do anything as it was God's challenge that he had put to them. But no one was curious enough to ask questions about disability or even attempt to help, so they were just left alone. It was also a time where it wasn't rare to see neglected disabled people. If you tried to speak out, you were either at risk of being killed or being locked away in a cage or prison. The year 1552 BC marks the first recorded findings of mental illness as it was called then from the Therapeutic Papyrus of Thebes. This document dates back to the ancient Egyptians; it was the first-ever medical record of its time and before doctors were around, this was vital for keeping people well. It is said that the Egyptians had mental and physical disabilities as we know today. They had conditions such as depression and dementia. If you think about it, it's a miracle how this document still exists as they didn't have any historians recording the lives of the Egyptians in particularly disabilities. There's an untold story in ancient Egypt that dates back 3000 years ago involving a dislocated mummy of a child of ancient Egypt. The child had skeletal dysplasia, which dates back to 1342–1197 BCE. There have been other studies that have shown that there have been findings of scoliosis. It is believed to be the daughter of King Tutankhamun who was having a disability in this time period. However, there were many people who believed that if a person had a disability, they were closer to God because of the challenges they had to go through because of the disability. They also believed that if you had a disabled person in your house, they would scare the demons away; the Egyptians were ahead of their time.

In 1552 BC, the Greeks and the Romans held a sense of self-image, which they believed to be the ideal human type, and that every human must look like this in order to fit in their society. Both the Greeks and the Romans saw themselves superior to other races, if you looked different or were not up to their expectations, then already you would be marked down in their society. This was also a time where people could call you an idiot if you weren't intelligent or couldn't do much to help the community.

Around the Fourth Century BC, new theories started coming to play as people assumed the causes or reasons for having a disability. At this time, if you had seizures or fits, people would guess that they had been the touched by the finger of God; the disabled were considered sacred. Hippocrates in 460–357BC, the father of medicine challenged this assumption by speculating 'that seizures were the result of a physical cause, not a divine intervention'. Hippocrates believed that the cause of epilepsy was due to the inexperience of well-being and was in the hands of man rather than in the hands of the Gods.

For children with disabilities in the ancient era, these weren't the best of times to be disabled. In Rome, children with disabilities were treated as objects.

Children who were blind, deaf, or mentally ill were publicly persecuted and it has been reported they were thrown in the Tiber River by their parents. Some children born with disabilities were mutilated to increase their value as beggars. Other children born with disabilities were left in the woods to die, their feet bound together to discourage anyone passing by from adopting them. In the military city of Sparta, the abandonment of 'deformed and sickly' infants was a legal requirement. It also wasn't uncommon for the rich to buy a person with a disability to either entertain them or to be their servants so that they would be keeping the house for them. These new ideas marked a point in history as the pinnacle point as the stigma towards disabled people began and even today, the teachings and the lessons that came from the ancient Greeks and Romans exist. Throughout the Middle Ages, the Roman Catholic Churches provided refuge for those in need which was most likely for the poor and for disabled people.

Later on, orphanages, hospitals and homes were built for the blind. In 787 AD, the first asylum was established in Milan which was for abandoned infants. In these tough times, the only way that these children could get out of these asylums was to be bought by a wealthy person, otherwise you were left in living conditions where most children died. Idiot cages were another thing that were used to display and humiliate disabled people in the major cities of Rome. If they were lucky, they were bought by the rich; if they weren't, then they would only be left to starve and die in these cages. After the rich bought a disabled person, they had the task of entertaining the public but if they couldn't, then they would be sold and to be put into a cage again and were never given a second chance.

Some people who were really disabled and were seen to be a lost cause were shipped off to other lands. Some countries would pay sailors to take these individuals away so that they weren't seen as a burden to their society. Countries like Italy, France, Belgium were the most common to follow in this act. A lot of people at this time thought by keeping the able-bodied people in and keeping disabled people out would create a perfect society, which would also create a one-way society which meant that if you didn't fit into their rules, then you were going to be out in a ship to set sail to the unknown. If only they knew that not a single person is to be blamed for the cause of disability, but our genes are. You can't help but think that if they knew, they would've been able to stay in their hometowns to be a part of their society.

Chapter II
Disability in Britain and Europe

1050–1485

During this period similar to the ancient era, this time was hard if you were disabled. If you were seen having a disability, some people in the community saw them to have a curse, other people thought that you were closer to God and that you would go to heaven sooner, since religion played a vital role in medieval communities. When it came to being treated, a lot of the treatments were at local churches as they believed that it was teachings from God that would eventually make you feel better. The treatment was basic food, clothes, housing the poor. There wasn't a government to help people with disabilities. Most lived and worked in their communities, supported by family and friends. If they couldn't work, their town or village might support them, but sometimes people resorted to begging. They were mainly cared for by monks and nuns who sheltered pilgrims and strangers as their Christian duty.

The Outbreak of Leprosy

Leprosy was one of the first disabilities to be documented in Britain. In the beginning of the fourth century, there was an unknown disease which was killing people without knowing what the cause was. It was not until the eleventh century when we realised that it was an endemic by 1050. In its extreme form, it can cause loss of fingers and toes, gangrene, blindness, collapse of the nose, ulcerations, lesions and weakening of the skeletal frame. Reaction to the disease in English society was complicated. It could be seen as a punishment for sin, it was also believed similar to what the Egyptians did. People who suffered from it seemed to suffer like Christ, therefore were closer to God. They also believed that after their enduring torment when they died, they would directly be sent to heaven.

In 1247, it was an exciting year as one of the first few hospitals were being built to help treat the outbreak of leprosy and other disabilities such as blindness and physical disability. The first mental institution was originally the Bethlehem Hospital in the City of London. But then later, it would be called 'Bedlam'. Almshouse Homes were built in the medieval period onwards, to shelter the elderly, disabled or other people considered unable to look after themselves.

1501–1660

At the beginning of the sixteenth century, there was a change in Britain. All the places that the disabled people went to, whether it was at church or a special institution, they were ruled over by the Roman Church and when King Henry VIII split from the Roman Church, it was devastating for people in need because he wanted every building that was ruled by Rome destroyed. This led to thousands of disabled people to come to the streets of London and other cities. In the sixteenth-century Britain, it was so easy to get diseases because hygiene wasn't of high standard as it is today. King Henry VIII hired the fearsome Thomas Cromwell and his men on horseback to destroy the Roman churches. Everyone was fearing for their lives when they heard the sound of horses running, booming the ground. The nuns and monks that once ran the medical churches would soon be no more as they ran out of the churches; if you were brave enough to stand against Thomas, you would either be tortured or killed. Thomas's men torched both the churches and medical workhouses mainly on the roof of the church showing no mercy; you could see the smoke rise in the atmosphere and across London; you could see each church being lit in the distance in the night sky you could see for miles. This event that took place was during the course of a week and many people lost their lives. The only reason why this started was that it was wrong to be disabled.

Members of the community were outraged at what had happened. Even the able-bodied people were in full support at the treatment that disabled people got from the king. A petition was put towards the king in 1538 to allow disabled people to be removed off the streets and into an institution but Henry VIII ignored the people of England. It would take another 30 years before a building would be made for them. However, as the king did nothing, the community started to come together. By 1539, caring for the disabled was no longer seen as a religious act but now a civic act which meant it was no longer up to God to look after them, but it was up to the people around them to do so. Men who were rich started to help fund buildings that would be their hospital; it wasn't the kind of hospital we know today but it was really basic back then, but still, it got disabled people off the streets. The reputation of the community grew as everyone clung together and helped one and other.

Towards the end of the sixteenth century in London, a massive new project went underway from Parliament to start building new buildings which were called Almshouses, hospitals of their day. This was huge for the disabled as 30 years before, they were practically left on the streets. A series of new laws would soon change for disabled people across Britain; if you couldn't work but you were seen to have been born with a disability, then money was soon to be coming for them by the state. However, if you were seen as a beggar that didn't do anything, then you wouldn't get anything, and you were just left homeless as they didn't do much for the homeless in those days.

This is a story which even shocked me, and I hope you'll enjoy it too. Towards the end of King Henry VIII's life, Henry wasn't particularly happy with his illnesses. The king was suffering from puss-filled boils and gout (inflamed arthritis in his feet) due to his obesity. He was also experiencing a form of depression not only ever since his jousting accident but because he had these horrible illnesses for a while now. He needed someone to lift up his spirits, someone to make the king laugh again. Well, this story I'd like to call the King's Last Servant. A man called William Sommers born in Shropshire in those days, he was what they called a fool. Today, he would be known to have a learning disability, but despite that William was asked to perform his comedy act in front of the king in his court.

William started performing and not many people were expecting this to go well because Henry had been unhappy for some time; to everyone's amazement, the king started laughing and started to enjoy William's performance. Henry was so impressed by William's sense of humour that the king offered him a place inside his court where he would also have clothes and food. This would be the king's first entertainer to have a disability. William was absolutely delighted to work alongside the king. Although throughout his comical career, not all of them were a success, William was asked to do a dare by Sir Nicholas Carew to say to Queen Anne Boleyn he made sexual jokes about her and then calling his daughter Princess Elizabeth a bastard, somehow William got away with it his act, even though Henry had threatened to kill William with his own bare hands. But Henry did like his comedy a lot; in fact, he did mention that he was his favourite jester (joker) at the time; which was a huge compliment. William could help Henry distract him from his injuries with his comedy which provided a well-needed remedy for the king until 1557. When the king died, William was sad, but despite the king's death, William was still allowed to stay in the king's court and he was still going to be paid the same as before. William would continue to entertain the royal family until Queen Elizabeth I came to power; her coronation was his last performance in front of the royal family, then he decided to retire from his duty in 1559.

1660–1832

New explanations were now challenging the idea that God caused madness and disability. The madness was no longer seen as the main cause of the disability of the soul. It was the loss of reason, and this could be restored with the right treatment. A disabled person had suffered a misfortune, not been sent a divine message, and they deserved charity. Support for people with disabilities was a Christian's duty, which you might be given in the form of relief, which was money from the state to treat the sick, the elderly, and disabled people. The disabled people for the first time were now getting some independence from society by getting this money. It was giving them the chance to get better health care and also a chance to be more accepted in society. Later on, in this period, new hospitals in England were now in full swing after the great fire of London. In 1666, rich traders and merchants used this as motivation to start to build new buildings which were hospitals and new housing. This building programme would turn out to be massive, the fire blazed through London at such a fast rate that 436 acres of land were affected, 13,200 houses were destroyed and 87 out of 109 churches were destroyed. Astonishingly, this programme was set up immediately after and it took only ten years to finally have London fully recovered. This was great for disabled people to finally be treated in hospital.

The Rise of Mental Asylums

The 1830s-2000s

During the course of the nineteenth century, asylums and workhouses were built to help look after disabled people across Britain. Asylums were built to treat mental health problems, the treatments that they used were extreme; in fact, they made patients worse. The staff that worked in the asylums was not even trained in the profession; the treatments that they thought would work were all done on assumption, rather than the safety and welfare of patients. The reason was that medical science was going through a revolution which started in the late eighteenth century, more doctors were coming up with new ways to treat physical and mental disabilities.

At the beginning of the nineteenth century, treatments were limited. But that didn't stop doctors from trying new things. They didn't necessarily work as the side effects afterwards would often make the mental and physical health of patients worse.

One of the first treatments that were available was ECT Electroconvulsive therapy, which worked by sending electricity to the brain, which made the body go into epileptic seizures. During the seizures, doctors would have to hold the patients down to the bed so that the patient wouldn't injure themselves during the treatment. Doctors at the time thought that the brain would change or get rid of the thoughts which cause depression. We know now that epileptic seizures don't change our brain patterns or thoughts; the ECT just makes you have an epileptic seizure, nothing else.

At the time though, some patients did feel that their depression had improved, others felt that it didn't do anything or had gotten worse. ECT was reported cause short-term memory loss but doctors were sure that patients could regain their short-term memory back. Unfortunately, this wasn't the case, so they continued to use this treatment whether they liked it or not. ECT continued to carry on treating patients for the next 70 years until another treatment came along which seemed to be more popular-fluoxetine also known as Prozac.

It was a revolution when it first came out in the 1980s although ECT was still available and could still be used; fewer and fewer patients were using it as doctors were relying on tablets to treat depression than to have your brain electrified by a machine, it proved to be a lot safer. Another treatment that was used for treating mental health was insulin injections which proved to be highly dangerous as a large amount of insulin would be injected into the body which caused the blood sugar levels to go up so high that the body wouldn't be able to cope. It caused heavy sweating and even led to a coma. In the 1940s and 50s, doctors believed that comas could cure schizophrenia; in the late 50s doctors published medical papers that were proving that the insulin wasn't helping schizophrenia at all, so doctors slowly stopped using it and went on to using ECT instead.

The third treatment that they had to offer was lobotomy. This procedure was one of the worst treatments for patients. It involved making incisions in the frontal lobes of the brain which is meant to release pressure to help treat depression and anxiety. As a consequence, some patients were left paralytic after the surgery. Some patients had their memory affected. They couldn't realise who their closet family and friends were. With their memory being affected, they had to learn everything again-how to brush their teeth, how to put clothes every morning.

In the 1970s, a politician called Enoch Powell tried to close down these asylums but they continued to treat patients this way and nothing was done. Twenty years later, in 1990, Margaret Thatcher the prime minister shut down all the asylums and eventually one by one, patients were discharged into the community. Every patient left with a memory of torture of what they went through in the asylum but at least they knew that they were free. The last asylum to close was called High Royds in 2003. This was a start for all of these patients to mingle in society and begin a new chapter in their lives.

Victorian Attitudes to Disability

In 1848, ten years after Queen Victoria was first crowned, religious advice from leaflets featured disabled people, not all advice was there to help, as many people didn't want to help at all. It wasn't uncommon to see people laughing or be violent towards the disabled while walking around the streets of London. There was an article in the leaflet which gives us an idea on how people treated them at this time which reads, 'Some boys laugh at poor cripples when they see them in the street. Sometimes, we meet a man with only one eye, or one arm, or one leg, or who has a humpback. How ought we to feel when we see them? We ought to pity them'.

The writer had a sting in the tail for the jeering boys as cripples might be made 'bright and beautiful' by God on judgement day.

It was common for the able-bodied men and women to laugh and not care for the disabled people, particularly if you saw them beg for money. Wicked able-bodied children who laughed at them. There was no protection by law for disabled people, so whoever abused them simply got away with it. Some disabled people would die when violent people would attack them. This became the blueprint for Victorian attitudes towards disability—a combination of fear, pity, discomfort and an idea of divine judgement.

Living in the Community

Even before Victorian Britain and across Europe, it was a popular idea that in order for disabled people to live in the community, they'd have to go to an asylum or workhouses. This was used as a form of treatment if a family couldn't look after their disabled child. If they got better, then they could come back home and live in the community but more often than not, most disabled people wouldn't come out again due to the lack of good quality health care that was around for disabled people at this time. Social investigators at the time didn't really show mercy in describing them. Social investigator Henry Mayhew (1812–1887) described the disabled beggars of the streets of London in 1862, as 'idiotic looking youth shaking in every limb' and the 'crab-like man without legs strapped to a board (who) walks upon his hands'. Not much sympathy for disabled people at the time. But it wasn't all doom and gloom in this time period. Some disabled people prospered. James 'deaf' Burke (1809–1845), also known as 'the deaf one', rose from poverty to become a world champion prize fighter. Henry Fawcett (1833–1884), blinded as a young man, became postmaster general in 1880; he introduced the parcel post and the postal order.

Education Specialises

Despite there being stigma towards disabled people, there was a glimmer of hope as children and young people with a disability started to receive education. English and literacy played an important role in allowing disabled people to become more accepted in British society. Learning English gave deaf and blind people a voice which they could use to communicate with both able-bodied and the disabled which was ground breaking at the time because it created a benchmark to allow disabled people to make their mark on British society for the first time in history.

On 12 January 1838, the London Society for Teaching for the blind was formed by a man called Tom Lucas. He came up with his own way of teaching the blind by embossed text (3D text) on paper which allowed blind people to read by feeling the shape of letters of the alphabet and this lead to developing words once the student got used to it. So, by the 1840s, education for disabled people sky rocketed to new heights, as education for disabled people became in high demand and so more schools were built across the country. Two new schools were built and opened by the London Society for Teaching, in Exeter and Nottingham and in 1866, the Worcester College for the Blind for the blind sons of gentlemen became the world's first higher education programme for disabled people. In the 1890s, local authorities were empowered to set up day schools for blind, deaf, 'defective' (children with learning difficulties) and epileptic children. By 1899, there were 43 schools in London alone teaching 2,000 children. Children who had a learning disability would be sent to a mental asylum in the absence of such schools. These schools allowed children to get an education, so that life in the asylum wasn't the inevitable route as it used to be.

1914 to Now

After WWI, certain attitudes in Britain needed to change as society still invested in the old-fashioned behaviour of thinking that disabled people were nothing but a burden on society and believing that disabled people offered nothing in return. Shortly after WWI, society managed to change and not just in Britain but across Europe. Suddenly, there was medical advancements on plastic surgery so that when injured soldiers were in need of a prosthetic leg or arm or even surgery on the face, more doctors performed these surgeries so that these war heroes could try and live a normal life as possible. During the war, many soldiers experienced the most horrific scenes of violence which gave them severe shock which is also known today as PTSD (post-traumatic stress disorder). These soldiers were rushed to the hospital. After the war, soldiers got both mental and physical illnesses. More help was available for physical illnesses but for mental health, little treatment was available. Doctors at first thought of letting them rest in their beds and give them electroconvulsive therapy for help.

Later on, doctors saw that it was having more of an effect on the body than the mind, which was proving that it wasn't working at all. Doctors turned to sergeants of the British army as a new idea to help these men. They thought that exercise might do the trick, so they tried exercise routines as part of their training; with very little success. They might as well have sent them back to war again as the exercise routines reminded them of what they went through in the war. So, then doctors had another idea of getting them to talk about what they went through which was more successful than the exercise routines, but it still wasn't a cure for PTSD or severe shock. However, it was a start in trying to find new treatments for mental well-being of the soldiers that came back from the war. Not only did PTSD affect soldiers that fought but also medics that were out there in the frontline, during the war. This made doctors stuck on how to treat someone with a trauma that hadn't even gone to war but having the same symptoms.

People who suffered from trauma often ended up in the asylums to try and get better treatment as that was the only treatment option available at the time. People with mental health were often pushed out of society and shut away either in an asylum or in their homes as they were seen as fools.

The Royal British Legion

Supporting Our Disabled Service Men and Women

Before the end of WWI, there was a need for an organisation to help provide a service for ex-servicemen and women that fought in war. On 15 May 1925, an organisation called the British Legion was born. At the time, the national federation, Comrades of the Great War, the National Association of discharged sailors and soldiers, Officers Association worked in four sectors of the army. General David Haig and Thomas Lister, a soldier who fought in the First World War came back badly wounded. Nevertheless, he never let his war wounds get in the way as he wanted to provide a better service for ex-servicemen. They helped bring the four organisations together to create one organisation for war soldiers. Tom became the first-ever chairman of the British Legion and General David Haig was the first-ever president until his sudden death in 1928. The British Legion got its royal status in 1971 which is known as the Royal British Legion today.

In the 1930s, attitude of people towards disabilities started to change, as soldiers who came back from WWI started a change in the way that we view disabled people and mental health. As disabled people are just like every other person; just that they look different doesn't make them any less human; disabled people still have the same feelings and emotions as us all, so we need to look out for them. When soldiers came back, they taught a lesson that anyone can have a disability whether it's physical or mental; age, gender, or background did not matter. But disability doesn't define people lives; it just might take longer to do certain things or think to do things differently altogether for the disabled.

In the 1940s, plastic surgery was undergoing a huge revolution. Surgeons were using surgery to reconstruct parts of the body that had been blown off in the war like the face, arms legs, and prosthetics were used to put on soldiers who lost their arms and legs so that they could walk again. Employers were advised to hire disabled people as a way to help them recover from their injuries and get back into the workplace. They didn't work full time, but part-time work was what they did as it was also known as sheltered work meaning they weren't doing main roles in the workplace, but they could do the side roles in the workplace. One of the major employers that employed a lot of disabled people was the Royal British Legion poppy factory. It employed ex-servicemen and women to help make poppies to help remember the soldiers that died in WWI and WWII and many other wars that have happened after. The British Legion had been incredible in helping the wounded, helping the lost and protecting their futures. This was also the first time that disabled people were even seen not only working but out in society. As to previously, they weren't even allowed to go to the shops to get food because of stigma.

You could say that the war had a really negative effect and yes thousands of people died fighting for their country but it also had a positive impact in raising awareness like no other to bring disability to the forefront, in that disability can affect anybody, no matter where you come from. It revolutionised health care and changed our perceptions of disability and that's certainly something to take from WWI.

You're probably wondering why I'm putting this in well the Royal British legion was one of the first charities to help people with physical disabilities in the UK and it paved the way for so many other charities to follow in helping disabled people.

Chapter III
Founding Fathers of Disability

Hippocrates

Hippocrates
370–460BC
The Father of
Modern Medicine

You can't really learn about the history of disability without knowing this particular person. Hippocrates also known as Hippocrates II because his grandfather was called Hippocrates. However, he really paved the way for modern medicine today as he was one of the first people to believe that disability wasn't caused by sins, tales or the Gods. His theory was that disability was caused by natural reasons like the environment, diet and living habits. Hippocrates learnt his craft from his father and grandfather as they were physicians too. Hippocrates and his followers were the first to describe many different illnesses we know today. For example, he noticed that somebody had clubbed fingers which is a sign for lung cancer and heart disease. They were also called Hippocratic fingers as well for this reason.

He was also the first-ever documented chest surgeons of this time. He was the first person in Ancient Greece to cut open and dissect the body to see what's going on internally. At the time, this was a very taboo subject and not many people were allowed to do this. He had the idea to drain out liquid along the chest wall abscess using lead pipes which are still used today, although there are other ways than lead pipes to drain the fluid but this treatment is still used today. Hippocrates also was the first to categorise different illnesses which he called acute, chronic, endemic and epidemic, kind of similar to when you go into hospital and a doctor will ask you on a scale of 1–10 how bad is the pain or illness. Acute is only the really minor illnesses and chronic is bad but manageable; endemic is bad, the patient needs medical help and epidemic is close to incurable (dying).

Hippocrates's Theory

Hippocrates had a theory-he thought the body was made up of four humours (liquids), used four components that measured how someone was feeling based on the method:

Yellow Bile

The people with high amounts of Yellow Bile were very passionate; they could get angry a lot, but they were very lively.

Black Bile

These were people who had chronic depression and very sensitive, but they were very artistic.

Blood

This is the main humour out of the four. People with high level of blood were confident, joyful, optimistic, expressive and sociable.

Phlegm

People with high levels of phlegm were deep thinkers, fair, calm, willing to compromise, and hard workers.

He believed in order to keep healthy, you had to keep the body in balance. This happens when the patient is left hot and dry, hot and wet, cold and dry and cold and wet environments which cause these liquids to imbalance by keeping out of extreme environments should improve symptoms as well. Hippocrates wrote over 60 books; historians later combined his work into one book called the Hippocratic Corpus. He strongly believed that resting and decent food would be another way of keeping healthy. One of his famous quotes in one of his books is 'let the food be the medicine and let the medicine be the food'. He also believed that doctors should keep a record of the patient's medical history which makes it easier to know what the patient has been through in the past and he couldn't stress enough on how important it was to observe and look at the body so that you knew what the symptoms were and what to do to get better.

The Hippocratic Oath

Even till this day, there is some debate on whether he wrote this but in the Hippocratic Corpus, there's an oath which future doctors and physicians to read or say in order for the patient to have complete trust with the physician and to keep professionalism the main priority while taking care of all patients. The oath has been rewritten over and over to suit the different cultures around the world. No one knows how he died but he left an everlasting legacy which changed our perception of modern medicine and disability to not think of it as a curse but as a condition which is caused by natural or biological causes. After Hippocrates's death, it seemed that the idea of the cause of disability was still Gods and it went to the ancient Roman times; it's only been since science has advanced that Hippocrates ideas were finally proven.

Galen was born in the city of Pergamon which is today known as Bergama in Turkey. His father was Aelius Nicon who was an architect, builder with an interest in maths, astronomy and logic. His mother was a very hot-tempered woman according to Galen in his diaries. He would often compare his mother to the wife of Socrates (Xanthippe) who had the same personality traits as his mother. One day, his father had a dream that his son would one day become a doctor and he would be helping people get better. Soon after Galen's father died which was a devastating blow for Galen but nevertheless Galen began studying medicine at the age of 16 as he wanted Galen to become a doctor or a philosopher. His father left him quite a substantial amount of money at the time and he used it to travel abroad to learn about different ways of life. This allowed him improve his knowledge on medicine which involved going into medical schools in Alexandria in Italy. He gained practical knowledge in a gladiator school where he learned how to be a gladiator surgeon. For Galen, this was an ideal place to learn his craft. In 162AD, he travelled to Rome where he soon became famous as a doctor to the Roman emperor and teacher of other doctors.

Galen
130 AD-210AD
A Greek Physician,
Surgeon and philosopher
who used Dissection as a
way to understand the
body

Galen believed in Hippocrates's idea on the four liquids of the human body, but he also had ideas of his own that could help the imbalance of the liquids. For example, if you are suffering from too much phlegm, then you should eat something that's dry and hot like peppers or chilli which is called the theory of opposites.

He is also famous for the dissection of animals such as apes and dogs but the most famous one was a pig. He cut into the pig's neck to teach the role of nerves to the wider public. We all know that nerves are from where electrical messages travel from the brain through the nerves to different parts of the body to move. He wanted to prove that nerves control the voice box as well as his said to the audience 'if I just cut this nerve here' not a single sound came from the pig again. This allowed Galen to prove that the main organ in the body isn't the heart like the ancient Egyptians believed but it was the brain that controls our bodies, which led him to believe that an animal's anatomy is different from a human's. Galen used dissection as a way to understand how the body worked which is why he later told his students that whenever they have the chance to dissect a dead corpse, take the chance.

Not all of his ideas were correct as he thought the left kidney was higher than the right; correct for an ape but not for a human.

What really made Galen famous though was his books. He wrote more than 60 books on human anatomy but only 60 of them are still around today. His books were so convincing that they were a main source of medical information which lasted for 1500 years.

Galen tried to show his students how different the body fitted together into a well-designed whole which came from the idea that we are made perfectly and that there must be a creator that builds us from above. This idea was taken seriously by the Christian church thinking that God created human beings.

Another idea that Galen had which not everyone agreed on was that he suggested that the mind was the same as the body, and went in to suggest that if you keep the body healthy, then you will keep the mind healthy. Many people disputed this idea but they couldn't disagree with him as he was seen as one of the greats in the ancient medical world.

Throughout Galen's life, he was a formidable physician who looked after the great Roman emperors of his time. He looked after the Roman Emperor Commodus until he died of the plague (The Black Death). Galen was permitted to stay on as the emperor's physician and he looked after Commodus's successor Septimius Severus. Galen praised the emperor for keeping a stash of drugs in his secret case that was only to be opened by Galen for the emperor to receive them when he was in need of them. But dark times were hitting Rome as the plague was an epidemic and Black Death was killing 2,000 people a day. Miraculously, Galen wasn't affected but Emperor Septimus Severus died shortly after the epidemic. Galen continued to write about treating the plague (not to describe it) as he didn't want people to worry about getting the horrible disease as you could imagine there was a tremendous amount of fear. Any knowledge that Galen would give to the people would just make it worse. Galen concentrated mainly on the skin, somebody who was affected by the plague would get terrible ulcers, so he would find remedies and ointments as a way to treat them. There wasn't much else that he could do because by the time that Galen saw the people that were affected, they were really close to dying and Galen just allowed them to die and to be at peace.

Like I mentioned before, Galen managed to survive the Black Death epidemic and he spent his final days in Rome. There are mixed opinions on how and when he died as some people think that he died at the age of 70. Other records suggest that he died in Sicily at the age of 87 which would've made him live another 17 years. As this record is from a book that Galen wrote called *On Theriac to Piso,* most people suggest that this theory is more likely, but we will never truly know.

Legacy

What a truly remarkable legacy that Galen has as he used his surgical abilities to go deeper into understanding the anatomy of both animals and humans and his books are timeless classics as some physicians today still read them to get some medical information. He survived the plague and his commitment to writing would shape the way we know medical biology today.

You may think that Galen didn't do much towards people with disability but his knowledge helped pave the way for everyone to feel better again and more importantly, how we should all treat everyone else, disabled or not depending on the severity of the condition there was only so much he could do.

This is why I've chosen to put Galen as one of the founding members of disability.

Chapter IV
Cerebral Palsy

Cerebral Palsy has been around since ancient times.

First documents found in early 1800s but the disease is a lot older as scientists have found it in mummies in Ancient Egypt.

For those that don't know what this condition is, cerebral palsy affects the brain's messages to the muscles. This can also lead to painful muscle spasms, or stiff muscles; it also affects coordination and leads to uncontrollable shaking. Motor skills are affected, meaning a delayed response to when you want to move your arms and legs making it hard to walk, hard to eat because the muscles around the mouth are hard to control, hard to speak, hard to pick up objects like a crayon or a fork. In the worst cases, it may lead to seizures.

That's a brief idea of what a person with Cerebral Palsy has but who came up with it? Who was the first to talk about it? Well, to find this person we need to go back in time to the eighteenth century in London.

Dr William John Little was born on the 7 August 1810 in London, where his father owned an inn. William suffered with a club foot and was partially disabled by polio. He completed his education in England before continuing his studies in France. He could speak French fluently; in 1826, at the age of 16, he returned to England, to start a two-year practice in a pharmacy. When he was 18, he started medical school in London Hospital. Soon after, he became a teacher, teaching anatomy, physiology, and pathology.

In 1832, when he was 22, he was admitted to the Royal College of Surgeons; however, his first attempts to get into the college weren't successful which led him to leave England to travel to Berlin in 1834 to continue his medical studies.

During his studies, he met a pioneer in tenotomy called Luis Stromeyer. He was one of the first orthopaedic doctors in the world that found treatments for feet deformities. Tenotomy involves the division of a tendon by cutting through it in the back of the heel to help release and lengthen them so that the patient will have more movement in the foot and then a patient could start the process of

learning to walk again. Stromeyer could see that William had a club foot, so he offered to treat him by operating on it. The operation was a such a success and Stromeyer inspired William to continue his studies on foot deformities.

In 1837, aged 27, William earned himself a degree in treating feet deformities at the University of Berlin. William decided to return back to England later that year. He performed the same operation as Stromeyer did on a 15-year-old boy which was his first patient in London. More and more patients were coming asking to be treated. So, he expanded and set up his own private practice in 1839. William also wrote a book about his work which was called *On the Nature and Treatment of the Deformities of the Human Frame*, which made him more popular across London.

In 1840, William Little got his desired job as a surgeon at London Hospital In the same year, in Bloomsbury Square, he opened the world's first hospital that was solely for treating orthopaedic disorders (feet deformities), which later came to be known as the Royal Orthopaedic Hospital of London. He wrote of his experiences of treating young children in his papers, describing the suffering that these children went through 'spasticity and stiffness of extremities' deformities of upper and lower extremities; he saw a lot of children experiencing weak muscles and in other cases inflammation of the muscle was too painful to touch and paralysis.

Little has compared the stiffness that his patients had to tetanus spasms. The connection between the above and perinatal disorders became more and more clear to him. As his experience grew, little classified children's disorders into groups. Of particular importance was the connection between bone, joint, and muscle deformities and disorders of the neurological system. His studies later on showed him that not only this disability was a physical one but also a mental one. His theory for the cause was a baby was born prematurely or the mother had a difficult delivery. In particular, Little thought the cause maybe to do with if the baby was starved of oxygen before birth which he called (perinatal asphyxia) in his papers. When the brain is starved of oxygen, tiny cells die in the brain, then we lose function not only in our brain but our bodies as well which was the reason behind the spasms and tremors.

Little was the first person to explain in detail the mechanics involved in muscle contractions, particularly (weak muscles). Additionally, little described cases of pseudo hypertrophic (a form of muscular dystrophy) at around the same time as Edward Meryon and before Guillaume Duchenne. The more Little observed and experienced, he was becoming more aware that the surgical treatments of cerebral palsy that they had at the time had its limitations. The initial fascination with tenotomies gave a cautious approach; this was caused by Little's observations that some treatment corrective in theory, in fact, could make symptoms of cerebral palsy worse rather than better which impaired children's motor function. This was an exceptionally new idea at the time when orthopaedics was going through the period of post-operative disaster.

This knowledge was reflected in his major work on this topic. Based on what he observed of over 200 patients little presented his main ideas in 1861 in a meeting of the obstetrical society of London. His views stirred a heated debate. He highlighted that the disease was caused by problems during pregnancy, and delivery. He underlined the impact of such conditions as placenta praevia and prematurity. Little believed that cerebral palsy resulted from post-partum asphyxia (brain damage) which distorted the blood flow and, in this way, damaged the child's brain. He was convinced that the cause of the disease was lack of oxygen during delivery. While rejecting the hypothesis of the impact of injuries during delivery, Little also described in detail different types of paralysis—hemiplegia (one side of the body is paralysed) diplegia (sometimes known as 'little diplegia'), because he came with the idea which affects the whole body affecting the legs more than the arms. and tetraplegia aka quadriplegia today, similar to diplegia all four limbs being paralysed, which starts from your spinal cord; it's caused by an illness or disease. He also pointed out the possibility of flaccid paralysis. He saw the link between a degree of paresis (muscle weakness) and a degree of mental illnesses in patients.

Little was one of the first to describe what is now called cerebral palsy even though he never used the term in his work. The first person to use the term cerebral palsy was William Osler in 1888. Sir William Osler wrote a book titled *Cerebral Palsies of Children*. Osler didn't refer to the disability as Little's Disease, as it was once called but instead built upon Little's work and added to it from his own scientific findings. Osler chose to base the term 'cerebral palsy' on the Latin words for 'brain' and 'paralysis'.

Sigmund Freud (1856–1939) He was a neurologist who described the changes to the brain with the types of paralysis and refined the concept of spastic diplegia.

In 1893, Sigmund is the first medical researcher to disagree with the theories put forward by Dr Little and Osler. Freud suggested that cerebral palsy was a brain-related disease that affected children before birth (not during or after as Little proposed). Freud also associated various disorders, including intellectual disabilities, visual disturbances, and seizures with cerebral palsy. Nowadays, cerebral palsy is caused when abnormal activity happens when the brain is growing. If the brain was be damaged or just grow differently or not completely, then a child would develop cerebral palsy in the womb.

William John Little-Later in Life

Little resigned from his post at the London Hospital, but he still practiced as a surgeon and continued his research. He retired because of his progressing deafness and moved to Ryarsh in Kent where died on 7 July aged 74

William's Legacy

William John Little married a woman called Eliza Templin. They had 11 children, seven survived into adulthood. Two of his sons continued his orthopaedic mission, and in 1918, one of his son's Ernest Muirhead Little (1854–1935) became the first president of the British Orthopaedic Association. The techniques used today in the surgery of muscular dystrophy were developed by Stromeyer and Little. William Little was one of the first to work in the field. Between neurology and orthopaedics, his work continues to have influence in both fields today.

*Sigmund Freud
(6 May 1856 to 23
September 1939)
Psychiatrist who
believed that Cerebral
Palsy starts during the
growing process in the
womb*

Sigmund Freud was born on 6 May 1856 in the Austrian town of Freiberg; it's changed since then it's now in the Czech Republic.

When Sigmund was only four years old, his family moved to Vienna, the town where he would live and work for most of his life. In 1881, Sigmund received his medical degree. As a medical student and a young researcher, Sigmund's research focused on neurobiology, which focuses on the biology of the brain, the nervous tissue of humans and animals. After he graduated, Sigmund set up his private practice and began treating various psychological disorders. Sigmund didn't see himself as a doctor; he saw himself as a scientist who wanted to understand the journey of human knowledge and experience. Early in his career, he became inspired by his friend and colleague, Josef Breuer who helped a mentally ill patient learn to talk. Josef and Sigmund worked a lot together, but Josef ended their working relationship as he felt that Sigmund was focusing too much on sexual origins of a patient's neurosis and wasn't willing to see his own viewpoints. Meanwhile Sigmund continued to define his own theories.

In 1882, Sigmund got engaged to marry Martha Bernays; the couple had six children together their youngest, Anna Freud who went onto become a psychoanalyst herself. Towards the end of his life when he should have been happily retired, his world turned upside down. In the beginning of March, there was news that the Nazis were coming for Austria by 15 March 1938. The Nazis had completely invaded Vienna by this point. His daughter Anna even got arrested because their family was Jewish, so by this, point Sigmund knew that he had to escape. So, he flew to England with his wife and children. Sigmund was battling mouth cancer which really led to a downward spiral of his mental health and he asked his doctor for a legal dose of morphine. As Sigmund came from a medical background, he got them. Few days later, he died at the age of 83 on the 23 September 1939 from an overdose of morphine.

Sigmund's Legacy

It is thanks to Sigmund that we know that cerebral palsy starts in the womb and to see how the brain and the mind truly work. You could say that Sigmund is one of the founding fathers of modern psychology as well a truly remarkable man.

William Osler
12 July 1849–29
December 1919
Founder of the name
Cerebral Palsy

William Osler was born on 12 July 1849 in a remote part of Ontario known as Bond Head. He spent a year at Trinity College in Ontario before deciding that he wanted a career in medicine. He attended the Toronto Medical College for two years and in 1872, received his medical degree from McGill University in Montreal. Like his fellow physicians, they trained and studied in Canada, but William chose a different path in choosing to study abroad in London, Berlin and Vienna before returning to Canada in 1874. He joined the medical facility at McGill University. A year later, he was promoted to professor. William was elected a fellow of the British Royal College of Physicians in 1883, one of only two Canadian physicians at the time. In 1884, he left Montreal for Philadelphia to become professor of clinical medicine at the University of Pennsylvania. It was not until 1887 that the term cerebral palsy came to light from a book that he wrote called cerebral palsies of children. The book summarised William's research and medical papers on cerebral palsy. He also provided an insight into treating CP including therapies that could help manage the symptoms better.

In 1888, William was recruited by John Billings to be a physician-in-chief of the soon-to-open John Hopkins Hospital and also a professor of medicine. William was the second appointed member of the original four medical faculty following William H Welch and preceding Howard A Kelly and William Halsted.

William Osler revolutionised the medical curriculum of the United States and Canada. He had ideas based on what he experienced when he travelled to Europe at it was leading the way at the time. William adapted to the English system whereby he was teaching future medical students to attend the patients' needs at the bed side. He believed by doing the practical work while studying with paperwork would the best way in teaching medical students. William also introduced the German system which suggested one-year apprenticeship followed by several years of residency with increasing clinical responsibilities which isn't very different from what we do today.

In 1905, he accepted the Regis Professorship of Medicine at Oxford University which was at the time the most prestigious medical appointment in the western medical world. He left Maryland with warm feelings for Hopkins Hospital knowing that his sixteen years spent had laid solid foundations for the future of Hopkins medical students. Throughout his life, he was a great admirer of the seventeenth-century physician and philosopher Thomas Browne. In 1919, at the age of 70, William sadly passed away in Oxford on the 29 December. It was suggested that he died of the flu which England was experiencing a flu which happened to come from Spain (Spanish influenza epidemic). His wife Grace lived for a further nine years before suffering from a series of strokes.

Sir William and Grace's Ashes now rest in a niche in the Osler Library at McGill University. William and Grace had two sons; one died shortly after birth but their other son, Edward Revere Osler was mortally wounded in combat during WWI at the age of 21 during the Third Battle of Ypres (The Battle of Passchendaele). At the time of his death in August 1917, he was a second lieutenant in the British royal field artillery. Lieutenant Edward Osler's grave is in the dozing ham military cemetery in West Flanders Belgium.

Legacy

William really paved the way for medical care in America and Canada and the name cerebral palsy; we certainly owe gratitude to his work.

Cerebral Palsy Today

With the use of modern technology and modern medicine, cerebral palsy is no longer a problem as it once was. People with cerebral palsy have a far better life now. Without Little's hard work, it would've been a lot longer to figure out what CP is and for that, we should be grateful to him.

Around two or three children for every 1,000 babies born develop cerebral palsy.

Around 764,000 people currently live with cerebral palsy, with 500,000 of those being children and teens.

Each year, 8,000 to 10,000 infants are diagnosed with cerebral palsy.

Around 1,200 to 1,500 pre-school aged children are diagnosed with cerebral palsy each year.

Cerebral palsy remains the most common type of the disorder, affecting close to 61% of all people with cerebral palsy.

Chapter V
Dwarfism

Mystery of Little People:

Going back 250,000 years, roughly to when we were homo sapiens (modern human), there once lived a very unique species of human, they were smaller only to be less than 4 feet tall and once lived across Asia, their last known place that they lived was the Flores Islands. This is where they get their name from. Moving on to roughly to early 2000s in Australia, a team of archaeologists dug out some old skeletons in an ancient graveyard; they were originally expecting to find just normal human bones, what they found was the oldest skeletons that happened to be dwarfs. It couldn't be a child because the pelvis and the joints were similar size to an adult's but the bones where the limbs would be were a lot shorter giving a clue that this was a dwarf. Throughout history, there's been a confusion among scientists to consider dwarfs as a totally different species of human. They dug out remains were ancient remains of little humans that lived in the Indonesian islands of Flores and they moved to Australia where the caves were. Now, considering that they were only 3ft tall, they could do extraordinary things, despite having a smaller brain than average height humans. This didn't stop them they had imagination and creativity like we have.

They battled Komodo dragons that were five times bigger than today. Homo floresiensis also had the ability to design tools like modern humans; they used sharp stones as knives to cut meat and food. They made fires to cook the food. Homo floresiensis worked in packs to get their pray like other species of human. One of the reasons why they were only 3 feet tall is that it was very hard to find the right nutrients for the body to grow normally and a lot of the times, it would've been hard to get the right amount of calories. Also, the humidity would've been draining on the body and genetics. Without the right nutrients to keep the cells in the body healthy and strong, they weaken. So, they evolved to shrink.

There's a debate that's still going on today that whether homo floresiensis are related to us or they are completely different species from chimpanzees.

Some scientists say that they were modern humans but with a disability; some say they had Down Syndrome; some say they had dwarfism, there are no definite answers to these questions but I have a theory.

Homo sapiens left their homeland in Africa and spread off in two directions—through one way went through Asia and the other was through India heading east to eventually get to Indonesia, where they also met with the homo floresiensis; no one knows if they were modern humans or descendants from another breed of human. For this part, we only have theories than answers but I think that as they were on the island of Flores and the conditions made them evolve to shrink set off early stages of dwarfism in our genetics meaning that the conditions on island life had a permanent effect on our genes, therefore dwarfism is still around today.

But the question is-did modern humans breed with homo floresiensis? Or did homo floresiensis evolve on their own to answer why dwarfs exist today which brings even more unanswered questions. To answer, we only have theories and ideas but if you were to ask me, I think that homo sapiens and the homo floresiensis did breed together not only so that our genetics were passed on but also to survive which would explain how they had an incredibly advanced brain for their size, to strategise like us, to imagine like us; it also explains how we have dwarfism today. Whatever answer you may have or what your gut may tell you, what an incredible story this is and one of the things I like about biology is that sometimes not everything needs to be answered sometimes we just need to embrace what we have an accept biology for what it is. Embrace differneciality as it makes our world more interesting and unique. Even I have to admit the story of Homofloresiensis is my favourite out of our human history.

Ancient Egypt

Let's move a little bit towards the future. In Egypt, dwarfs were treated really well. They worked as servants or a personal nurse to the royal pharaohs, they also treated the sick when in need. The Egyptians saw dwarfs to be close to God; they thought that they had a closer connection with God so that if the dwarfs helped out the Egyptians, then they would also be close to God. So, they acted as helpers for the people. Their role was to be in charge of families, home and even help with childbirth, as they thought that they'd make the perfect midwives since they were short and this would make easy to work with mothers on the floor. They were also personal nurses similar to modern doctors today asking people how they were and finding out ways to help make them feel better. If they worked alongside Egyptian royalty, then they were allowed to stay in the palace, get paid well and accommodation that anyone would dream of. Other dwarfs got the help of able-bodied people to build their own homes; that was if they could afford it. This was allowed as dwarfs were respected in Egyptian society. Dwarfs also had a variety of jobs from fisherman, to working with jewellery; they'd even go inside caves in search for gold. They entertained the Pharos through dancing and music, cracking a few jokes; dwarfs played a huge part in Egyptian culture, more than we realised, they were the secret to keeping the Egyptian legacy alive.

Dwarfism in Europe-Italy

Across Europe, dwarfs were treated differently than the ancient Egyptians. Europeans didn't believe that they had sacred gifts and were close to God. Across Europe, dwarfs were often sold to the rich, also sold to the royal families of the United Kingdom, France, Italy and Greece were the main countries; these dwarfs were called court dwarfs and they were used to entertain royalty and the rich. This job was the only job for a dwarf at the time to guarantee clothes, bed and decent food to eat otherwise dwarfs would often starve to death. Around the fifteenth century in Italy, a woman called Isabella d'Este was a wealthy woman who often bought dwarfs; she gave them jobs for entertainment and as artists who would entertain her and the public. Isabella's parents were extremely wealthy as well, and later in life, she married a wealthy man. She never looked down towards dwarfs. She saw them as mystical humans she adored; this is why she bought a lot of them. She even went as far as to re-designing their rooms, so they did not have to struggle in her palace. The stairs would be the right size for them to go up and down the staircases on their own. Even the ceilings were brought down to size for them. Not all dwarfs were used as precious gifts at the time but they were for Isabella. When her brother (Alfonso) was ill, she sent her favourite dwarf Matello to sing to him when he was in bed and danced, even performing somersaults as a way to help Isabella's brother recover. Isabella nursed her brother to health but despite her best efforts, he died which was heart-breaking for both her and her dwarfs. Alfonso was buried in the family crypt. Despite this loss. Isabella went on to become patron of arts, supporting upcoming new talents Mantegna, Titian, and da Vinci. She then asked all of them to paint a portrait of herself. She invited writers, artists, and poets to her home to exchange ideas and corresponded frequently with a variety of prominent figures, letters that now provide us with a rare woman's point of view on Renaissance Italy. During her time as ruler, d'Este also funded an ongoing school for girls. Isabella's palace the Palazzo Ducale at its time was the biggest building in Europe. She allowed her dwarfs to live with her in her palace until she died. Later in life, she became a ruler in her own right in the small city of Solarolo in 1529 until she died ten years later.

Dwarfism in France

Dwarfs in France were treated very similarly to how they were treated in Italy. The royal family in France bought dwarfs as gifts which would have been expensive. The rich paid for them for entertainment purposes.

Dwarfism in Britain

In Britain, dwarfs weren't always treated with the best care, often starved and left in a cage waiting to be bought by the rich and royalty, so they could have a happier life.

Dwarfism in Spain

In Spain, things were totally different. Dwarfs were adored by the Spanish royal family and the rich. They worked as servants, they got paid for it. And for the first time in the fifteenth century, some dwarfs got access to an education which average people never had. This led to jealousy from other servants who worked the same hours as dwarfs but not necessarily got an education; there was conflict from time to time, so dwarfs had to be careful on who they spoke to when it came to able-bodied people.

Dwarfism in America

In 1939, over in America, there was a film that really showcased dwarfs in a different light. A film called the *Wizard of Oz* was a huge leap for dwarfs in modern society; it really allowed people to see dwarfs in a different way. It was the first time that dwarfs weren't seen as outcasts. For the first time, dwarfs worked on the same project as able-bodied people. Nearly 30 years later in 1957, things changed again in America.

In 1957, there was a revolution that began that would change the way we would all think about dwarfs forever and that was the movement of the Little People of America (LPA) originally founded by Billy Barty. He was a dwarf himself but he had a platform which was his acting and he wanted to provide equal rights for dwarfs like the able-bodied people, not only in the film industry but also in everyday life. Dwarfs weren't taken too seriously in the 1950s. A lot of people in those days saw them as people who belonged to a circus or on a stage. A lot of dwarfs in the 50's would get called horrible names in the street like midget. But Billy knew that dwarfs were capable of much more than acting, so he came up with an idea of making an organisation that would help other dwarfs in America. Billy wanted to make it possible for other dwarfs to get a job in the film industry mainly but also have success in everyday life as well.

The very first LPA meeting was held in Reno, Nevada. At the time, there was just Billy and 20 other dwarfs that signed up. The association just grew and grew over the years and it became stronger than ever, with an estimate of 6,000 members in America. The LPA offers dwarfs the ability to have a decent education which was and is revolutionary because dwarfs before this time were often put into schools for learning disabilities. Even if a dwarf was bright and intelligent, they wouldn't be allowed to go to a mainstream school or even express their intelligence like able bodied people. The LPA also gave dwarfs a better chance of gaining employment. By giving them tips in interviews, and disability rights to ensure that discrimination did not stop dwarfs from getting what they deserved. The LPA offered valuable medical support and advice for both dwarfs and parents because no dwarf was the same due to the different causes and types of dwarfism. For example, Achondroplasia has different side effects to let's say Pseudoachondroplasia, what I mean by side effects is that being a dwarf, they can get pain in their back, hips and joints as the legs of dwarfs are bowed, so they have difficulty in walking. The most common case of dwarfism is a condition called Achondroplasia; it affects 90% of dwarfs where the bones aren't developed properly. There is a gene called FGR3 which stands for fibroblast growth receptor 3, which is located in our chromosomes; this gene causes a mutation in our bones which slows down the process of normal growth in the womb and lack of cartilage to form the bones, particularly, in the longer bones in our skeleton such as the humorous.

Who Discovered Dwarfism?

Dr Pierre Maroteaux Unknown DOB-1926— Death Unknown French Physician who discovered Dwarfism

Dr Pierre Maroteaux was born in France in 1926 and he was the first person to discover dwarfism as he discovered a theory that achondroplasia was a genetic condition. Pierre was a scientist that had a specialist team around him.

He worked hard to find out the cause for dwarfism and they eventually found that there must be something in our chromosomes as the cause. Maurice Lamy worked with Pierre to study the order and number of chromosomes in patients who have Dwarfism. It wasn't until 1994 that the gene FGR3 was discovered by another doctor called Dr John Wasmouth for 99% of cases of achondroplasia which was a breakthrough in treating Dwarfism.

What makes dwarfs the way they are is that the FGR3 gene affects the bone growth structure. When they grow in the womb, the cartilage doesn't grow into bone, it just remains as hard cartilage which makes them short.

Dwarfism Today

One of the things that people with dwarfism still face today is stigma. Unfortunately, there is still the odd comment where a dwarf will get called names by others such as midget and many other negative names associated with dwarfism. Other struggle most of people suffer with dwarfism is that when you live in a world which is designed for taller people, everything is out of your reach and you constantly have to rely on family and friends to get the things you want for you; even having to rely on the kindness of strangers to get by. Living with dwarfism isn't necessarily independent as you are constantly adapting to a larger world around you. There is hope that we are starting to understand more about disability as a whole. I hope that one day we won't be calling them midgets, one day I hope that we can see their own uniqueness for who they are and not to judge them for their appearance; we should all be taking a lesson from that, dwarfs certainly have a proud history we should all learn about.

Chapter VI
Osteogenesis Imperfecta

(Brittle Bones)

At the start of this story, we need to go back to almost the beginning of human history where animals and humans lived side by side. It was at this time that we were living in caves. In Europe about 25,000 and 13,000 years ago, there was an ice age that swept the whole of northern Europe from England to France, Germany, Belgium, Poland, Denmark, Norway, Sweden and Finland. This was a time when our early ancestors (homo sapiens) were around and this ice age was so cold that it had an ever-lasting impact on us as a species. The ice age managed to block the sun's solar energy which caused our bones to become fragile because our bodies weren't getting enough calcium as the sun was our main source of calcium to make them stronger. It left an impact on us even today because it rewrote our genetic coding which now forms the mutations of brittle bones. The ice age was so bad that even evolution which is designed so that we become better, faster bigger stronger etc. could not save our bodies from bone deformities, so when the next generation of people came, conditions like osteogenesis imperfecta and dwarfism, skeletal dysplasia became more common. But then something else had changed-our skin. Our bodies managed to evolve so that our skin could change colour from black to white which helped us absorb more calcium as the sun wasn't as strong in Europe, compared to Africa or when the sun isn't as effective in the winter periods. So, you could say that this is the start of the white humans that would rule the world for centuries after that.

Osteogenesis imperfecta is one of the oldest disabilities in the human race along with dwarfism, blindness and being deaf. It's not quite the beginning of the human race; we were on the planet before the ice age, but it left an impact on our genes through evolution, which changed the direction of human history forever. I have a theory that our genes through evolution either the ice age created a gene with a mutation or that the ice age was so damaging that evolution couldn't repair the gene, therefore, brittle bones came to us through a mutated gene. Either way this is how we got brittle bones; it doesn't just mark the beginning of disability but also holds the answer to how inherited disabilities can occur.

The First Mention of Brittle Bones

Our next adventure takes us on a different journey and surprisingly, brittle bones weren't documented in Ancient Egypt; as such it was more skeletal dysplasia which is a case of dwarfism but the earliest mention of brittle bones was in the Viking Period. I have to say this person is one of the most powerful rulers the world has ever known despite having brittle bones and that is Ivar The Boneless, which was his nickname but his real name was Ivar Ragnarsson. Born in modern day Scandinavia, he was the son of a Viking King who led many armies that built wooden boats and sailed the sea. He sailed to England like his father before him and followed in his footsteps to conquer England. Ivar's father Ragner Ragnarsson first took over England by invading York to which he succeeded. But the success wasn't to last as he tried to fight further south, the English armies got the better of him and eventually killed him and the myth goes that the English threw the body into a pit of snakes, leaving them to feast. When Ivar heard the news, he did not cry or shout; he was utterly speechless, in fact, he didn't react at all. The other Vikings shouted and were incredibly saddened by the news. But Ivar knew what he had to do. He planned months of tactics on what to do with his Viking warriors and set out on his own quest to kill the kings of England and claim it his second home. Ivar knew that he would need a stronger army, so he rallied a bigger army with his four brothers-Hvitserk, Ubba and Bjorn and the Great Heathen Army was born. Ivar also gathered more Viking warriors from Norway and Sweden to sail to England.

The Vikings had already claimed York as their land, so they travelled further south, to what was called Mercia at the time. But their first battle was in Nottingham. The king of Mercia begged to the king of Wessex who was Alfred the Great, and he offered to pay the Vikings away to which the Vikings declined and so they later on fought the king of Mercia which then led to their victory after they killed. They decided to perform the blood eagle on the king of Mercia as he had killed their father. It was a very painful death which involved cutting open the back while the person was still alive or dead and they broke the rib cage and pulled the lungs through the opening and sticking on the side of the body looking like wings. The Vikings then splits off into two armies to conquer more land at a faster rate. Ivar went up north to Scotland, then set sail to Ireland. But on the way, Ivar got ill but no one knows the actual cause of his death, but there were ideas that he died of a disease or infection or he died of brittle bones. The more likely case to happen was that he died from a disease while travelling to Ireland, we do know he didn't die in battle. He died in the year 873AD.

There are so many unanswered questions about Ivar-what he looked like? How bad was his brittle bones, did he even have it in the first place? We can only go by theories to answer this question, but I think he did have brittle bones otherwise he wouldn't have had the nickname boneless. The most common question is was Ivar carried into battle or did he fight individually? If you think about it, Ivar would be such an easy target if he was carried into battle because he would not only look different, but he'd also be exposed to enemy arrows. I think that Ivar would've trained so hard as a young boy to make his muscles stronger that he could move himself by crawling and being able to fight with a bow and arrow or a sword. A person with brittle bones becomes really strong if they work hard at it, as the muscles would support the bones. But exercise can offer benefits to bones as well; it can make them grow bigger, thicker, stronger. Ivar to me is an Incredible Viking for not letting his disability get in the way and he didn't let other Vikings rule over him either; he was a leader with extraordinary ambitions. This is why Ivar is certainly an important figure in the history of osteogenesis imperfecta.

Ancient Egypt

So, here we are again in Egypt. Osteogenesis imperfecta has been in Egypt from the start of the Egyptian Empire but there hasn't been much evidence to suggest that it was around at this time until a team of archaeologists dug their way through an old cave which was basically a tomb of mummies that once lived 3,000 years ago and one mummy stood out—that of an infant having osteogenesis imperfecta. No one knows what life would have been like living in Egypt with OI but this infant was probably killed as Egyptians didn't know much about brittle bones.

Sweden

In 1788, Olof Jakob Ekman and his team were the first to do some tests on the bones that were found from infants and research suggests that the infants had type 1 brittle bones which is a mild case of the disorder. From then on, scientists could now fully diagnose brittle bones in patients. This was ground breaking. But it still needed a name; it wasn't until a French Pathologist Jean Lobstein first came up with a name.

Jean Lobstein worked alongside Olof and he not only helped find out what this disorder was but what the causes were. Jean found through months of testing that this disorder was genetic, and he knew that when someone who had osteogenesis imperfecta type 1, the cartilage doesn't grow normally as it leaves bones to be vulnerable; even a fast movement of an arm could break your shoulder or arm when the baby was born. Jean was the first person to name the disorder osteogenesis imperfecta, but he also called it after him (Lobstein Disease). Osteogenesis simply means development of bone and imperfecta simply means imperfect. Our bones start to form just three months of growing in the womb. In chromosome 17, we have a gene called COL1A1 which is collagen type 1. It is the building block for our bone development during the growing process in the womb; in normal bone growth, collagen type 1 supports the proteins in our eyes, bones, skin normally, but in case of OI, the collagen isn't good quality or the quantity isn't enough to sustain the framework of the body which explains the reasons behind brittle bones.

Jean Lobstein
8 May 1777–7 March 1835
Who Discovered the genetics & the name of Osteogenesis Imperfecta

Denmark

Willem Vrolik
29 April 1801–22
December 1863
Who discovered that
Osteogenesis
Imperfecta starts in
the womb

In the 1850s, **Willem Vrolik** (Dutch Pathologist) studied ancient suffering. Willem was one of the first people to discover the disorder which he even went as far as naming Vrolik Syndrome and this is known today as osteogenesis imperfecta. Willem was born in Amsterdam 29 April 1801. Willem first got studying medicine at the University of Utrecht. In the Netherlands, he then went to Paris to further his studies. He got his medical degree in 1823 (aged 22) at the age of 28. In 1831, he then went on to becoming a professor of University of Groningen where he became a professor of anatomy and physiology. Then Willem travelled back to the University of Amsterdam, where he was appointed a professor in natural science, it would've given Willem the knowledge on gene mutations which would've proven vital for diagnosing brittle bones. Willem came across a condition where people found it ever so easy to break a bone. Through his research, he discovered that it was an impairment of ossification which meant that in the growing process, where reformation of the bone took place, an inherited condition that happened in the womb. To which he calls it Volrik Syndrome in his papers. Willem was also one of the pathologists to find the symptoms the same as Lobstein but also, he found that brittle bones was caused by a gene mutation which happened in the growing process in the womb. Willem discovered a very small infant being born. The baby was a little boy and he managed to survive for only three days. The skull was almost too big for his tiny body as the bones weren't formed correctly. The poor boy had a high forehead and small fontanel (the tubular bones) managed to grow of a normal length but they were slightly curved and very thin, so the ribs were thin and curved. Practically, the whole body had sustained more than one fracture. In 1993, the infant was re-diagnosed with osteogenesis imperfecta type 2 which makes perfect sense as the infant very shortly died because this type is the most life-threatening of them all. Willem discovered that brittle bones is caused by the growing process of the bone tissue in which the bones are fragile.

Willem's Legacy

The Vrolik Museum is named after his father Gerard Vrolik (1775–1859) and his son Willem (1801–1863). Gerard and Willem were both professors of anatomy in Amsterdam. Their Museum Vrolikianum was a private collection that was set up in their canal house. The collection included normal anatomy of humans and animals, but also anatomical anatomy and congenital defects. After the death of Willem Vrolik, his collection was bought by a group of wealthy Amsterdam men. They donated it to the University of Amsterdam. Although the collection was subsequently extended by several successive Amsterdam anatomists, the name Museum Vrolik remained. The Vrolik museum has been located in the Amsterdam Medical Centre since 1984. On display at the museum, you'll find malformations of babies from when they are in the womb and a very large collection of skeletons which Willem must've used to research about brittle bones disease or Vrolik Syndrome as he called it.

The development of babies in the womb can be followed closely at Museum Vrolik. In Vrolik, you can also see congenital malformations such as (cyclopia), which is a rare birth defect, Siamese twins. In addition, there is a large collection of animal anatomy. In Vrolik Museum, a collection that was built in the late eighteenth century, the nineteenth century and the first quarter of the twentieth century, the normal and abnormal building and development of the human body is a central theme in the museum. Both Gerard and Willem wanted to provide the answer to the public to the vital questions-How do we look inside? How are our organs and body parts are built? And where exactly are they? This was their life mission, so that medical science could advance further and save lives.

Willem received international recognition for his work and received a prize from the French Academy of Science.

Professor David Sillence: Professor of genetic medicine in University of Sydney. Consultant Physician to the Connective Tissue Dysplasia Clinic and Centre for Children Bone Health at The Children's Hospital.

David Sillence Unknown—DOB Australian Geneticist Who discovered the types of osteogeneses Imperfecta

David made an important discovery that changed the way we see brittle bones forever. He found a new way of measuring bone density type 1 to type 8 and he created a classification system which is basically the types of OI to make it easier to diagnose patients with the condition.

Types in Detail

Type 1 symptoms-Children with this type often make it through birth as it's only a mild case of OI but in other types, it can be more life threatening as some babies die at birth. But throughout life, your bones are always going to be fragile and prone to break, the joints are easily dislocated as well as they aren't formed to the connective tissue as somebody without OI. The joints can also be very loose as well; in some cases, the doctor will need to have routine check-ups to see if it's normal and not fully out of place; muscles can also be very weak.

This is due to the bones being fragile and as the bones are fragile, the muscles kind of collapse making them very weak. But there are ways around it. By therapy, physio exercises and sports. The skin can bruise easily as well which can be caused by a break but other cases, it can be due to a skin condition where the skin will just bruise for no reason. Height is also an issue with OI; it's different from person to person but you're more likely to have a height that is below average when you reach adulthood compared to people that aren't affected. In a lot of cases of OI, it is not rare to also have curvature of the spine (scoliosis) but luckily, the case isn't as bad as compared to somebody with scoliosis; they just tend to curve slightly. Your eyes are also in different colour as well the sclera which is the white sides of our eyes change colour and they turn blue with a grey tint; this is caused by the underlying choroidal veins which you can see due to the sclera being thinner than normal which again is due to the lack of collagen in the eyes. In some cases, hearing is affected but that's a rare occurrence, it is affected due to the bones not being strong enough around the ear causing them to collapse.

Type 2 Osteogenesis imperfecta is the most severe case. Usually when babies are born with this type, they already have broken bones because the bones are even softer than type 1. Babies with this type also have a soft skull so you have to be very careful in the delivery process in holding the head. Limbs maybe disproportionately small and their legs looks like frog legs as they are in a bowed position. The face is shaped triangularly; the body is incredibly small with a head that's almost too big for the neck to support it. This type is life threatening; also more babies die during delivery or after birth, doctors predict that they only live 3–4 months after birth before dying. There are so many factors as the body is so small and fragile. Most likely causes of death are not being able to breathe as their lungs are underdeveloped in the womb which means that they aren't big and strong enough to be able to breathe on their own. Like type 1, they still have tinted blue sclera in the sides of their eyes also.

Type 3 Osteogenesis Imperfecta: Bones can easily fracture as before, similar to type 2; they have a very small stature with their sclera tinted blue, sometimes, more purple than grey tint, they have loose joints like type 1. Their chest is barrel shaped that covers the lungs and heart; they also have triangular face, spinal curvature similar to type 1. Breathing problems can occur but it isn't as common as type 2 as the lungs are better developed. Collagen isn't formed in the right way. Overall, type 3 is a mixture of type 1 and 2; the symptoms are worse than type 1 but it has some better forms of type 2 OI but type 3 can still be lethal but at least there's a better chance of survival than type 2.

Type 4 Osteogenesis imperfecta: This type also ranges between two types but this time, it's between type 1 and 3 in severity, bones still fracture easily. But mostly children when adults will have stronger bones. They are shorter than the average person. Like type 3, bone deformities can be a range of mild to moderate. Other symptoms are barrel shaped rib cage, triangular face, hearing loss is possible, the collagen isn't properly formed.

Type 5 Osteogenesis imperfecta: This type is similar to type 4 in appearance and symptoms. Calcification of the membrane between the radius and the ulna leads to restriction of forearm rotation. Symptoms also include white sclera, normal teeth and the bones have mesh-like appearance.

Types 6,7, 8 of Osteogenesis imperfecta share many of the same features as before but these types are extreme as types 3&4; severe growth deficiency, extreme mineral deficiency, short stature, short femur and short humorous are common symptoms.

Is Osteogenesis Imperfecta Genetic?

These types are the final piece of the puzzle that we know as brittle bones today. Dr Sillence has also done a lot of work in genetics and actually found the gene that proved Willem Volrik's theory of the condition being genetic. In our 17th chromosome, we have a gene inside there called COL1A1 or COL1A2 which is responsible for providing us with collagen to help form the cartilage to build our bones big and strong. But in OI patients, this gene is mutated, therefore, the collagen isn't as good or there isn't enough collagen to support the bones, tendons, skin, and eyes in the body. But as OI patients grow towards teenage years and adulthood; we know through Ivar the Boneless and paralympic athletes that sport can play a major role in decreasing the symptoms, so strong muscles can ease symptoms. Through grit and determination, people with brittle bones have a proud history and we should always respect people who have it.

Osteogenesis Imperfecta Today

Today, the best treatment for brittle bones is available as we use a mixture of surgical innovation and calcium supplements to manage the symptoms of this disorder, which I know isn't a cure but we are getting closer to finding one every day to help those who suffer from it. More and more people are making sure that brittle bones doesn't affect their lives; with the power of exercise and a good diet, they can remain in good health to strengthen their bones as much as possible. More people are becoming famous and getting out there to spread their message that 'I have brittle bones but it doesn't affect me so it won't affect you if you have a dream you can achieve it to'.

Chapter VII
Motor Neurone Disease

Motor neurone disease is one of the difficult diseases anyone could have; it's not contagious. The ever-deteriorating condition effects the neurones that get sent from the brain through the spinal cord down to the muscles; over time, the muscle wastes away and the nerves in the brain are affected. Muscles in the throat are also affected which makes the patient lose the ability to speak. There are different types of motor neurone disease. There are four main types of the condition and two more recently discovered.

Types of MND

The first type is the most common type in the list which is called Amyotrophic Lateral Sclerosis (ALS). This type involves both the upper and lower neurones in the body and over time, the muscles waste away. When symptoms first occur, the patient may suddenly fall over for no reason or they may drop things. Speech may start to slur; as the muscles start to waste, the patient will start to lose control in moving the muscles. It's also the type that Stephen Hawking had during his lifetime. It's interesting though that the only part of the body that doesn't get affected or as affected is the eyes. The eyes have a different type of protein that manages to survive longer through the condition, which allowed Stephen to communicate though his right eye, then through a computer. When somebody gets diagnosed with ALS, their life expectancy is very short-only 2–5 years at the most. This rule doesn't apply to everyone. ALS can kill in 2 ways; the first one is that it can affect our lungs by weakening them. On the rare occasion, they shrink but it's different from person to person. The other reason that ALS can kill is through dehydration and malnutrition as the condition makes the patient lose the ability to swallow liquid and food.

The second type of motor neurone disease is called Progressive Bulpar Palsy (PBP). This type affects about a quarter of people. It affects both upper and lower neurones in the body. With PBP, this disease attacks the Bulpar muscles which is where the medulla is, which right at the top of our necks. This stops the messages that get sent from the brain to the muscles in this region of the body causing Bulpar palsy. When patient gets diagnosed with it, the life expectancy is between 2 months and 3 years. But everyone is different, and the condition is also different in how bad it is. With Bulpar palsy, the speech is slurred, face and jaw get weak, the tongue also loses its strength as do the arms and legs. Over time, the symptoms get worse and worse leading to needing 24hr care.

The third type is called Progressive Muscular Atrophy (PMA). This type is quite mild compared to ALS & PBP; it only affects the lower neurones in the body. Early symptoms may include clumsiness from the hands or feet but generally patients have better control over their hands because it only affects the lower neurones in the body. Patients with PMA have a longer life expectancy as well as it isn't as life threatening as the previous two. The average person can live up to 5 years.

The fourth type is called Primary Lateral Sclerosis (PLS); this won't come as a surprise to you that this type is also linked to another condition called multiple sclerosis hence the name; there is a difference between the two. This type is very rare; it's not often that doctors get to see this as patients suffer from stiffness from sclerosis and clumsiness from MND with PLS the two conditions are put together, and different patients have different experiences. Some get more symptoms of MND than Sclerosis or some might get more symptoms of Sclerosis than MND or they're even etc. If the patient has more of the sclerosis than the MND, then they are more likely to have a better way of life as the muscles won't waste away as much because it's a mild form. Some can also talk more than a patient with MND, but this is different from patient to patient. When a patient is diagnosed with PLS, the patient has considerably more years compared to ALS; the average life expectancy you get is 10 years at least.

The fifth and final type of MND is Kennedy's Disease also known as Spinal Bulpar muscular dystrophy. Kennedy's Disease is very similar to MND and often gets misdiagnosed because the symptoms are similar. Kennedy's Disease affects muscles wastage. There is 1 in 40,000 people who have the condition which is rare Kennedy's Disease. This is an inherited condition passed on by a gene which has mutated. It can be diagnosed through gene testing and other tests such as blood tests. Men who inherit it or are carriers of the gene only give it to their daughters whereas women give it to both sons and daughters. But women rarely develop any symptoms but if they do, they just get muscle cramps. Men however get a wider range of symptoms-muscle cramps, tiredness, twitching, difficulties in swallowing and speech. Over time, muscles get weaker and waste away which may affect posture and balance. With Kennedy's Disease, sugar and cholesterol levels may increase. Kennedy's Disease isn't yet associated as MND; however, it is supported by the MND Association as another type of MND.

What Is the Cause?

Sadly, no one knows what the cause is; research is still going on to find out what the cause is. But there are theories to suggest the cause. Environmental toxins and chemicals that enter the body which could affect the baby before it's born or during life. Premature ageing of motor neurones, loss of growth factors of the motor neurone which reduces the survival of the neurone considerably and genetic susceptibility. Most cases of MND occur spontaneously. These are said to be sporadic (occurring in shattered or isolated instances) without identified causes. There are theories that it could be inherited in the family. But studies suggest that only counts for about 10 per cent of cases. There is no evidence to suggest that it's contagious, so people won't have to worry getting it from somebody else. Damage to the nervous system in any form can lead to symptoms of MND.

Who Discovered MND?

Jean Martin Charcot
29 November 1825–
16 August 1893
Father of Modern
Neurology
Founder of Motor
Neuron Disease

One of the people to first discover MND is also known as the father of neurology, because he was the first person that took neurology to a place we know it today. That was Jean Martin Charcot.

Jean-Martin Charcot was born in Paris, France in 1825 at a time when the field of neurology had not been formally recognised as a specialty. He was also gifted painter in his spare time, who used his artistic abilities and strong visual memory to make associations about patterns of disease in the field of medicine and anatomy. At this time in the nineteenth century, mental health was seen as alien where many people didn't really know how to handle patients with a mental health issue, so there for left them alone. Jean wasn't interested in mental health issues as it wasn't seen as a good profession to be in but later in life as he became a physician, his attitude changed. He started to study about the brain and how it works; little did he know the aspects of mental health would entail. His father, was financially limited, so he took drastic action as he decided that the son who performed best amongst the four brothers in school would go on to receive higher education, a competition that Jean-Martin won, providing him the opportunity to enter medical school. He was fluent in four languages-French, English, German, and Italian, which enabled him to read the medical literature in these languages, which accounted for his well-rounded knowledge of a variety of subjects, including gerontology (diseases of the joints and lungs), and the anatomy, physiology, and pathology of the nervous system.

Jean was the first person to find out the symptoms of ALS at a time where it was very hard to prove a physician's theories. Through careful observations, and hard work, it took Jean a long time to find out the symptoms of this mysterious disease. He was the first person to diagnose ALS as a separate neurological disease as too many people thought that it was similar to multiple sclerosis at the time. Fifteen studies were conducted by Charcot between 1865 to 1869 and one of his colleagues called Joffroy found that lesions in the lateral column in the spinal cord leads to chronic paralysis and contractions without experiencing muscle waste, however, if the patient had chronic paralysis without the contractions resulted in muscle waste. This explains how patients' muscles get deformed when the muscles waste away. This study supported Jean's theory that the motor component of the spinal cord consisted of a two-part system. Jean didn't publish his study this until five years later in 1874 when his teachings were collected up into a final collection titled (completed work). In many countries, ALS is still named after the man himself as Charcot's Disease and rightly so. Numerous molecular and genetic discoveries have allowed better understanding of the disease. But it's Jean's theories and methods that stand alone as physicians today still use them; Jean's descriptions still remain unaltered two centuries later, which is an achievement in itself.

Jean Martin Charcot's Legacy

He was one of the first physicians to interview patients on their symptoms that would create a better understanding for him to fund better treatments for them.

Jean didn't just discover the disease ALS, but he also found other neurological diseases such as Parkinson's, multiple sclerosis and MS. He set up the world's first ever rehabilitation unit in Paris for mental health issues. He was the first physician to officially diagnose multiple sclerosis to patients.

Jean played a role in teaching future physicians such as Charles Babinski, and Gilles de la Tourette and Sigmund Freud who would go on to become one of the most famous physicians in medicine. He played a vital role in diagnosing patients with cerebral palsy.

Jean's most famous work was after his long hours of finding out the cause of a mysterious disease when he found the lesions of a patient on the top of spinal cord that would go on to diagnosing motor neurone disease; he always will be remembered for that and we can all thank him for it.

Is Motor Neurone Disease Genetic?

The chances of getting MND is very low as only 1/10 people get it from their family; it is more likely to be an environmental factor rather than hereditary. As Jean Martin Charot discovered that MND is the slowing down of the nervous system and whenever the body is experiencing a high level of stress, the nervous system can slow down because it's working so hard to catch up with the activity that you want to do. Let me give you other factors that can be the cause:

Trauma to the head.

If the nervous system is attacked or damaged in any way, then that could be the cause.

High levels of exercise.

Military service.

Exposure to chemicals or bacteria.

Exposure to heavy metals.

Not everything that's mentioned above can be said to be cause for MND as scientists don't yet know what the causes are for MND are but we have a lot of theories and ideas which do make the condition worse which is why we come to think that these are the causes of MND.

Treatment

In terms of treating MND, it's very hard because the nervous system is a complicated thing to work on; however, recently there has been some breakthroughs and they aren't cures, but they can help improve or slow down the symptoms of MND.

Stem Cells

So, stem cells have been really important in recent years in research because these cells are one of the most intelligent cells that we have in biology; they can find and serve damaged cells or areas of the nervous system and they can repair and restore the cells in the nervous system which can slow down the progressive nature of MND. Not only can they repair the nervous system but they can also restore brain function so that the brain can be healed so that the neurones and electric messages can run more efficiently and over time, the body will be healed by the brain. We still don't know the brain's full capabilities as the brain does have the potential to heal the body, but more research needs to be done on this matter. In the future, I hope we will be able to find this out. It won't only treat MND but other mental health issues as well.

Enzyme Q10 Vitamins

I know when I first read about a vitamin which could help MND. I was shocked myself; primarily these vitamins are responsible for giving us energy and protects our cells which can be damaged from oxygen, chemicals and bacteria. The reason why they are on my list is that research has shown that Q10 vitamins have the capabilities of slowing down the symptoms of MND which could help people who suffer the with the illness live longer. It won't cure them but at least it helps manage the symptoms better.

Healthy Mindset

Having a healthy mindset is very important when you have MND. If you have MND, your body muscles may slowly lose their function, but your mind is the only thing that stays the same throughout. The brain has the potential to heal the body through our thinking patterns. This is often called the placebo effect; if you imagine that you're going to get better or have a long life, you will have a long and healthy life because the placebo effect allows the brain to heal the body without any need of medicines or treatments. But of course, if it doesn't work, you may need a doctor, but the placebo effect is a very powerful tool. Having the will power to live everyday as if it's your last as Stephen Hawking did, this attitude helps you live longer. You can guarantee if the brain slows down, the body will follow it.

(Light Exercise)

Exercise is important when you have MND because you're keeping the muscles moving and strengthening the muscles has benefits for both the body and the mind. Even by today's standards, MND remains one of the trickier conditions to treat but there are ways you can slow down the effects of the disease so that people can live longer; more importantly, it wouldn't be a death sentence as it has been in the past. Always have faith in that with a positive outlook with MND, you can still have a normal life; you're just living it in a different way. Even if a carer or someone you know to assist in the movement, the muscles will still gain strength which is what patients need to slow down the progression of the muscles.

Motor Neurone Disease Today

Despite medicine advancing every day, there is still no cure for MND; however, there are ways of dealing with the symptoms that we are slowly understanding. In order to make further progress, we need to do some more research on the brain as I've said before we don't even know half of what the human brain can do.

Chapter VIII
Polio

Also known as poliomyelitis, the first cases of the virus was discovered in the early nineteenth century. The first person to discover polio was a British physician called Michael Underwood in 1789. He described the first clinical description that polio was a virus and that anyone could get it. Like many viruses, people were terrified of getting the virus; a lot of rumours were going round in America of a polio outbreak from 1910 and onwards. In most cases, polio can cause paralysis of the patient; only in severe cases, it can kill you. Polio is a viral infection which can spread very quickly from person to person if left untreated. It affected the United States the worst in the early stages. Polio did hit Europe, but many documents of polio were mainly found in America; the first announcement of the epidemic was in 1916. That year, there was 27,000 cases of polio and 6,000 people died from the virus. The virus can spread rapidly in your body; one minute you have a headache and then only one hour later, your muscles get stiff then paralysed; in other cases, patients lose the ability to breathe.

One of the first treatments that was available was a machine that was called the iron lung which was firstly made in 1929 by physician Phillip Drinker 1894–1972 and Charles McKhann 1898–1988 at Boston Children's Hospital, but it was still used to treat both children and adults with the virus. Harvard University published a paper at the time to say how successful the new ventilator was, the patient was in a container that helped you breathe. Doctors put oxygen inside the container which allowed the lungs to breathe. But nowadays, you'll just be put on the ventilator which is a lot better. The machine was first known as the drinker respirator and then later on, it was renamed as the iron lung as it would provide temporary and sometimes permanent breathing support which was essential for survival. When it comes to the symptoms, there are two parts of the virus-the paralytic and the non-paralytic virus.

The non-paralytic version is fever, sore throat, headaches, vomiting, fatigue, back and neck pain, arm and leg stiffness, muscle tenderness and spasms; in worse cases, meningitis, where an infection occurs in the membranes surrounding the brain. As for the paralytic version of the virus, it won't come as a surprise that these symptoms are worse even though that this only occurs in a very small percentage of those affected by the polio virus. Your muscles will get stiff or paralysed, severe muscle pain and spasms, loose of floppy limbs; one side is normally worse than the other. Paralytic polio may also be classed as spinal polio which affects the motor neurons in the spinal cord which causes paralysis in the arms and legs and even breathing problems.

Bulbar Polio-In this type of the virus, the neurones that are responsible for sight, taste and breathing are affected. Bilbao spinal polio causes both Spinal and Bulpar Polio. Luckily for us, polio had a very powerful enemy which would soon go all the way to find the cure of the virus.

Franklin Delano Roosevelt

The future president of the United States of America, but he wasn't president at the time. During the summer of 1921, Franklin was just enjoying a day of sailing in his yacht. But all of a sudden, he fell into the icy waters of the Bay of Fundy. He was very quickly saved out of the water by close friends, the next day he complained of lower back pain. So, he went for a swim to try and ease the pain but as the day progressed, his legs were getting weaker. The next day, he could no longer stand and hold his own body weight. When he fell ill from the virus at the age of 39, Franklin contracted the polio virus. On 25 August 1921, Franklin saw another physician Dr Robert Lovett who diagnosed him with infantile paralysis (polio). Franklin was completely paralysed from the waist down. But he never allowed the virus to take over his life; he had ambitions in politics. The polio was a complete secret from the public because he feared that no one would vote for him.

FDR did a deal with the press that there would be no pictures or videos of him in a wheelchair or getting in and out of a car. So, whenever he would get out of his car, the press would have no choice but to stop filming him. In 1927, Franklin launched one of the first rehabilitation units for polio in America called Warm Springs Foundation. Franklin spent a lot of time in the rehabilitation himself as a way to help manage his symptoms. He made sure that he stuck to his daily rituals of exercise and physio to help his leg muscles which certainly worked in his favour because he started to win the hearts of American people. He seemed like one of them, so when it came to the elections, he won in 1933 presidential elections. Franklin became the 32nd president of the United States of America.

America was going through an economic crisis; many people were homeless and had no money. This was known as the Great Depression. This still didn't stop Franklin finding a cure for polio. On his birthday, he made a broadcast that went out to the whole of the country. In this broadcast, he made a pledge to help find a cure for polio, so he wished that everyone would make a donation of one dollar, which most people did, and in the end, Franklin made enough money— $100,000—for Warm Springs Rehabilitation unit for people with polio which was ground breaking in itself as the death rate of the virus was decreasing. Not only that but the money was going to be put towards scientific research for a vaccine to prevent polio. Sadly, tragedy struck on 12 April 1945; Franklin Delano Roosevelt died at the age of 63.

Hope was yet to come though as a new doctor was in town and certainly made an impact. Dr Jonas Salk was hired by the University of Pittsburgh to develop a virus research program and received a grant to begin a polio typing project. He used tissue culture method to grow the virus. In 1953, Dr Salk made the first injectable polio injection. Like any new medicine, it needed to be tested, so a year later, over two million children were the first to try his new vaccine at Pittsburgh University. In 1955, news came out that Dr Salk's vaccine trials were a success by Dr Thomas Francis in a press conference in Michigan on 12 April exactly 10 years after Franklin died. Not only was this a huge day for science and medicine but also for Franklin as his fundraising for the vaccine paid off. The broadcast was both on television and radio, church bells rang all over the United States. As it was a scary time before and between 1955 and 1957 incidences of polio in America fell by 85–90%; not only was this the first step for America, but for the whole world as Salk's vaccine was transported all over the world and by 1979, the last case of polio was stopped, and the last case of smallpox was cured throughout the world.

So, what's the cause of this virus? Well, polio is the main cause of poliomyelitis and it's a member of a group known as Enterovirus C which is a species of Enterovirus which is part of RNA viruses. Ribonucleic acid is genetic material which is found in our RNA in chromosome 19.

Who Discovered Polio?

Karl Landsteiner
14 June 1868–26
June 1943
Founder of blood
types and
poliomyelitis

Karl Landsteiner was born on the 14 June 1868. Karl's father (Leopold Landsteiner 1818–1875) was a renowned journalist who was the chief editor of a German newspaper *Die Presse* but when Karl was at the tender age of six, his father passed away. This led to Karl having a close relationship with his mother Fanny nèe Hess (1837–1908). From an early age, his mother believed in hard work and she gave Karl the belief in working; throughout school Karl was a hard working student; he had a fascination in science and medicine. Karl graduated in his final exam in Vienna Secondary School. He then went on to study medicine at the University of Vienna and wrote his first doctoral papers in 1891. While he was still a student, he published his first essay on how diets affect the blood stream. From 1891 to 1893, he studied chemistry in different universities from Würzburg, in München and Zürich and he had a number of publications of this time period; some of them were helped by the professors who taught him.

Blood Types

In 1901, Karl found that there were three red blood types we know today as type A, B, O; he called blood type O as C at the time. He also found that blood transfusions would not harm anyone as long as two people had the same blood type. Hence, the reason why people give blood today. The first successful blood transfusion was performed in New York by Reuben Ottenberg at Mount Sinai Hospital in 1907. In today's blood transfusions, only concentrate of red blood cells without serum is transmitted which is important in surgical practice. In 1930, Landsteiner was awarded the Nobel Prize in physiology and medicine in recognition of his achievements. For his pioneering work, he is recognised as the father of transfusion medicine.

After returning to Vienna, he concentrated on the mechanism of immunity and the nature of antibodies. From November 1897 to 1908, Landsteiner was an assistant at the pathological-anatomical institute of the University of Vienna. Under his tutor Anton Weichselbaum, where he published 75 papers dealing with serology (studying blood serum), bacteriology (studying bacteria) virology (studying viruses) and pathological anatomy, he performed 3,600 autopsies in ten years for his doctor lecture qualification. In 1911, Karl was associate professor of pathological anatomy; during this time he discovered alongside Erwin Popper another Austrian Physician the infectious virus poliomyelitis and the polio virus. This ground-breaking discovery was the basis for the fight against polio. Karl and Erwin were both inducted in the Polio Hall of Fame at Warm Springs in Georgia in January 1958. Sadly, they never lived to see this award, but I'm sure they looked down from heaven.

Erwin Popper
9 December 1879–28 September 1955
Worked alongside Karl Landsteiner and is the Co-founder of Poliomyelitis

Polio Today

Polio is thankfully under control, thanks to the polio vaccine, thanks to dear Franklin who helped to raise money to beat it. Since 1988, the cases of polio have reduced 99%. It still hangs around in only three other countries-Afghanistan, Pakistan and Nigeria; they don't have a vaccine because they can't afford the treatment or just can't get access to the vaccine. Luckily, in recent years, we haven't had an epidemic in the west but there's always a risk of it spreading as the virus only needs one child to have it, so it can spread worldwide if it's not controlled. However, polio statistics are doing rather well and may it remain this way.

Chapter IX
Meningitis

Meningitis is a condition where swelling occurs in the meninges (outline of the brain) and the spinal cord, which can kill within hours if the case is severe. There are reasons on what causes meningitis. There are three main categories which are the cause-bacterial, fungal and viral. There are 50 different bacteria which causes meningitis. The bacterial case is the most severe case of meningitis but it's not as common as the viral meningitis; if left untreated, the bacteria can make the condition really serious. The inflammation in the outline of the brain can also have side effects such as headaches/migraines, fever and a stiff neck. Most cases of the condition are in the United States where most cases are caused by a viral infection which is easily treated with a meningitis vaccine. Let's see what's the cause of the bacterial meningitis. Bacteria that enters the bloodstream and travels to the brain and spinal cord. It can also happen when bacteria directly invade the meninges. This may be caused by an ear or sinus infection, a skull fracture, or in rare cases, after some surgeries.

What are the bacteria called?

Streptococcus pneumatic (pneumococcus)-This bacterium is the most common cause of bacterial meningitis in infants, young children and adults. It mainly causes pneumonia or ear and sinus infections. Luckily, this can be easily treated with a vaccine which helps prevent the infection.

Neisseria Meningitis (meningococcus)-This bacterium is another leading cause of bacterial meningitis. These bacteria commonly cause upper respiratory infections, but it can also cause meningococcal meningitis when they enter the bloodstream. This is a highly contagious infection that affects teenagers and young adults. It can cause an epidemic in school, colleges and universities and military bases; basically in places where there's a large number of people. But again, a vaccine has been made to treat the symptoms.

Haemophilus Influenzae (haemophilus) Haemophilus influenzae type b also known as (HIB)-These bacteria were once the leading cause of bacterial meningitis in children, but new HIB vaccines have greatly reduced the number of cases of this type of meningitis.

Listeria Monocytogenes (listeria): These bacteria can be found in unpasteurised cheeses, hot dogs and lunch meat; pregnant women, new born, adults, and people with weakened immune systems are most susceptible. Listeria can cross the placental barrier and infections in late pregnancy may be fatal to the baby.

The History of Meningitis

Meningitis has been around longer than most of us know; it has been around even when ancient medical papers were written. The earliest time period for this would be the ancient Egyptians. Meningitis was around but not many people documented it at the time. It wasn't until years later Hippocrates first mentioned that there were people looking really ill but not knowing what the condition was. This condition was making people surfer and eventually die. In the eighteenth century, a Scottish physician Sir Robert Whytt 1714–1766 in Edinburgh was the first person to discover the symptoms of what he called tuberculosis meningitis. He's also remembered for doing a lot of research in the nervous system. He believed that the nervous system was responsible for our reflexes as we know today whereas before him, physicians just thought that reflexes were in the arms and legs. The first symptom that Robert came up with in his research was the swelling in the brain. He called it the dropsy in the brain; he thought that it was caused by an infection which could spread from person to person. This was also fatal in this time as many people died from tuberculosis meningitis until the invention of chemotherapy treatments and antimicrobial medicine. Robert Whytt was so before his time that his findings were only theories and he never lived to see the final diagnosis take place. But his papers still inspired future physicians and worked out that his theories were right 100 years later.

Dr Robert Whytt
6 September 1714–17
April 1766
Described the first
symptoms of Meningitis

The first case of meningitis was recorded in Geneva in 1805 by **Gaspard Vieusseux** 1746–1814 and Andre Matthey 1778–1842 in Geneva and Elisa North 1771–1843 in Massachusetts. Meningitis was an epidemic at the time and it was bad in the United States though there were some cases in Europe as well. In Africa, the first outbreak was in 1840; the epidemics in Africa were more common in the twentieth century. The first major epidemic was in Nigeria and Ghana in 1905–1908 in which large amounts of people died from the disease. This was the first evidence that linked bacterial infection as the cause of meningitis. This was written by Austrian Bacteriologist Anton Vaykselbaum who described the symptoms of meningococcal bacteria in 1887. Heinrich Quincke 1842–1922 used a new technique of lumbar puncture in 1891 which helped him provide early analysis of cerebrospinal fluid which was the swelling on the spinal cord which can affect motor neurones. William Mestrezat 1883–1929 and H Houston Merritt 1902–1979 compiled a large series of studies in meningitis and they found the organisms that caused meningitis. These were identified in the late nineteenth century and included Streptococcus pneumonia, Neisseria meningitis's, Haemophilia influenzas.

*Gaspard Vieusseux
18 February 1746–
21 October 1814
Founder of
Bacterial
Meningitis*

Treatment

In 1906, the researchers noted that horses could be used to create antibodies against the meningococcal bacteria. This was developed further by American scientist Simon Flexner. This was a start of a revolution in fighting against meningitis. Simon Flexner dramatically helped save lives with meningococcal in the late twentieth century with vaccines for meningitis that were caused by a virus they were being developed. This vaccine was called the Haemophilus Vaccine Haemophilus influenza type B (HIB) in other words. This vaccine dramatically dropped the death rate for this type of meningitis which nearly got rid of all cases in the UK and Europe.

Is Meningitis Genetic?

Well, a recent study has shown that before we are born, meningitis doesn't develop in the womb. However, our DNA can sometimes make the symptoms develop further and worsen over time. This happens when a certain gene in a chromosome mutates similar to the other disabilities I talked about. Meningitis is not an inherited disease; we can't get it from our parents directly; however, there is new research which suggests that there are certain genes which make us more likely to get meningitis than others A study was published back in 2010. Researchers did tests on 1,500 people who had meningitis and 5,000 who did not, and the results came that meningitis isn't inherited but the immune system is made differently regardless of families or siblings. This is because of these genetic gene mutations it creates and shapes the immune system differently from others which makes the patient very vulnerable to getting meningitis. Our immune systems most of the time are made normally but in this rare case of meningitis which may explain that in some people, the immune system can defend off the bacteria without any problems and for others, they can deteriorate very rapidly.

Meningitis Today

Today there are one million people that are affected by meningitis worldwide, roughly 350,000 people die from meningitis every year. It is very hard to spot in the early stages as the symptoms can often be well hidden. It is also hard to decide what the type of meningitis it is to give the right possible vaccines to treat the condition. If the patient survives into later life, there is a high chance of experiencing life changing events:

Loss of vision (in one or both eyes).

Loss of limbs due to septicaemia.

Deafness.

Brain damage.

Learning difficulties.

Seizures.

Even though we have yet to see a cure, going back in time gives us some insight into how far we've come into understanding meningitis as a whole. In the future, we will be looking for hope as research will advance to find out the possibilities of finding a cure for meningitis.

Chapter X
Paralysis

Paralysis has been around for a lot longer than we think; paralysis has been around since ancient Egypt. Funny enough, Egypt was where the first name for paralysis came from it's a name, we still use till this day 'paraplegia' which was the first description of injury of the spine about 3,000 BC. People at this time had problems treating injuries of the spinal cord as knowledge was limited; this was the most common cause of paralysis at this time. The spinal cord is like the brain's railway system where the brain sends messages through the spinal cord to the muscle to move. In Egyptian times, people with disabilities were not discriminated as they believed that when someone who had a physical or mental disability, they thought that they were closer to God. Life for someone with paralysis would've been restricted in the sense that you may have been bed bound or house bound; families with a disability in this time did get help from the pharaohs by lending some money to improve the family's wellbeing. Moving ahead into ancient Roman times, things couldn't be more different as if you had a disability, your status through society's eyes would be lowered and you wouldn't get any help from strangers or from the state as people would be scared to get the condition themselves. Life expectancy wasn't high at this time for people with paralysis as the disease was common and very little food and water was available to survive. It would be considered old if you reached the age of 35. Education was limited too in Roman times as it only for able-bodied people. People with paralysis were more than likely not to have an education. Or if they were lucky enough, they'd be put into a school alongside those with special needs (learning disabilities).

Paralysis is where a muscle or muscle groups weaken or completely lose function. This is where the messages from the brain that travel through the spinal cord from the nervous system get damaged or the route is disrupted in some way. Paralysis isn't life threatening but it's certainly life changing. There are several causes.

Stroke.

Tumour.

Trauma (caused by a fall or a blow).

Multiple sclerosis (a disease that destroys the protective sheath covering nerve cells).

Cerebral palsy (a condition caused by a defect or injury to the brain that occurs at or shortly after birth).

Metabolic disorder (a disorder that interferes with the body's ability to maintain itself).

Sir Charles Bell
12 November 1774–28
April 1842
First described the
symptoms of Paralysis
and founder of Bell's
Palsy

In some cases, you can be born with paralysis.

Nothing in terms of treatment was really done until the early nineteenth century when a Scottish physician Sir Charles Bell first described the symptoms of paralysis. Sir Charles was born in Edinburgh. He was the fourth son of Reverend William Bell who was the reverend in the Church of Scotland. Charles attended a prestigious high school known as the Royal High School (RHS) 1784–1788. Charles wasn't the best student according to his school reports. However, he decided to take the leap of faith and follow his brother's footsteps for a career in medicine. In 1796, he enrolled into the University of Edinburgh where he first started as a surgical apprentice helping his older brother. Bell also attended lectures in spiritual philosophy and also anatomy classes.

Bell chose a course on the art of drawing to refine his art skills. Bell was also a member at the university's medical society where he even did a speech at the society's centenary celebrations. In 1798, Bell fully graduated from the university and went straight on to the Edinburgh College of surgeons. He taught anatomy and he performed surgeries at the Edinburgh Royal Infirmary. While developing his talents, Bell decided to combine anatomy and art together; he helped his brother illustrate one his first books called the *Anatomy of the Human Body* in 1803. Charle's stay in Scotland didn't last much longer although he wasn't involved in his brother's feuds in the infirmary but he offered a deal with the staff by offering 100 guineas and his museum of anatomy in exchange for him and his brother to stay at the royal infirmary. Sadly, the deal was rejected. Charles then decided to make it big in London the following year.

In 1811, Charles published a book called a *New Anatomy on the Brain* which in its self was ground breaking. In the book, he talked about how neurological messages get passed from the brain through the spinal cord and into the muscle in order to move the arms legs, eyes even the mouth. To prove his methods, he chose to test it on a rabbit by cutting open its back and looking at its spinal cord. He analysed it by feeling and cutting small bits to find out what would happen if the spinal cord was damaged. He found if the spinal cord is damaged in any part then the neurological messages can't flow through the cord like it should and therefore the rabbit and also humans lose the ability of motor function in the limbs.

At the time, this new idea got mixed messages as new ideas came to light at this time; the idea that the brain sends neurological messages would've been seen as absurd. Later on, Bell was heavily criticised for carrying out this experiment on the rabbit. Plus, the idea was rejected at the time; they thought that Bell didn't have enough information or proof that the spinal cord passes messages to the limbs to allow movement. Despite the criticism, Charles still studied on the brain and he published a new book called on the nerves. It talks about the experiments he carried out over the years. These experiments led to a new arrangement of the nervous system. He found that paralysis can also affect one side of the face; he named this disease Bell's Palsy which was a huge discovery as surgeons before thought that if you cut the nerve that would help cure the problem. Bell's Palsy gave future surgeons the knowledge to know how neurological messages, and the nerves inside our muscles are key to how our bodies move on a daily basis which is vital for treating paralysis today. Charles Bell may have got lots of criticism throughout his career but he provided the blueprint on paralysis that in itself is a legacy that will live on forever.

Treating paralysis

In the early nineteenth century, surgeons started to treat paralysis by cutting the nerves because they believed that the nerves were responsible for being paralysed. But it wasn't until Charles Bell that surgeons decided to think of new ways on treating the condition. Today, we treat people with paralysis with physical therapy with a routine of exercise to try and build strength in the legs and arms which doesn't cure it, but it helps manages the symptoms. In some cases, though people have achieved walking normally by sticking to the regime. Some don't, depending on how bad the paralysis is at the start. There are other ways to make life easier. As technology is advancing every day, there are mobility aids which are always helpful such as manual and electric wheelchairs, scooters and supportive devices which are helpful for people at the start of their physical therapy such as braces, canes and walkers. Recently, there are voice-assisted computers which can allow people to communicate without moving.

Is Paralysis Genetic?

Parents can't exactly give their children paralysis through genetics directly. However, when the baby grows in the womb, there is always a chance of getting paralysis when a gene mutates which has nothing to do with the parents. The gene mutation that's responsible for the cause is called ALS2, its location is in our second chromosome in position 33.1 which is further down the second half of the chromosome.

Paralysis Today

Today, we use modern technology to help improve the symptoms of paralysis. The use of modern wheelchairs enables paralytic patients to be mobile today. Physicians and rehabilitation units are there to help improve the patient's condition. This may not cure paralysis but at least help the symptoms. There are 50,000 cases in the UK and Ireland of paralytic patients. In America, a study was carried out in 2013 they found that there's a 1 in 50 chance of suffering from paralysis which leaves an estimate of 5.4 million people in America that suffer from paralysis. Across Europe, there's more than one billion people that live life paralysed. In Asia, it's considerably more where health care is harder to get, and countries are considerably poorer which makes the numbers stack up; it's even hard to get a wheelchair. I remain hopeful that one day technology will be able to help the people in Asia.

Chapter XI
Epilepsy

Epilepsy is a neurological condition where the brain's electrical messages explodes with electrical currents all over the brain causing the body to shake uncontrollably. Most of the time, you are unconscious, but some people have seizures when they are conscious, some have non-epileptic seizures. There are many causes of epilepsy:

Born with it due to lack of oxygen before birth.

Headaches or migraines.

Head trauma.

Lack of sleep.

The autistic spectrum.

Brain conditions such as strokes, tumours, brain damage etc,

Extreme changes in temperature.

Epileptic seizures can vary from person-to-person on how severe they are. Some seizures aren't very long 1–2 mins or 5–10mins any longer than 5 minutes then you'll need to phone an ambulance

Epilepsy can have side effects after a seizure.

Lose eyesight or a change in vision.

Bitten tongue.

Blacking (losing awareness).

Passing out (losing consciousness).

Confused or memory loss.

Feeling distracted or daydreaming.

Can't talk normally.

Short term memory maybe affected.

Fatigue.

Please take comfort in knowing that it's rare to experience severe side effects after a seizure; the most common ones are tiredness, biting your tongue and confusion. As I speak from personal experience from having epilepsy in the past (controlled now) it's rare to lose your sight and it's rarer to lose memory permanently. I've put them in the list for knowledge and educational purposes.

The history of epilepsy pretty much dates back to the beginning of human existence when human and animals roamed the earth side by side. The first reports of epilepsy can be traced back to ancient Egyptian times in a country known as Assyria which is known as Syria today. There are multiple references of epilepsy that can be found in ancient texts. Hippocrates (father of modern medicine) describes in his book sacred disease; inside it describes the first neurosurgery procedure which was called craniotomy which involved breaking the skull to get to the brain. Hippocrates said that the procedure should be done on the opposite side of the brain of the seizures which would prove to be inaccurate. During this time, people believed that the cause of epilepsy was swallowing too much phlegm (mucus) which we now know isn't the case. It wasn't until the eighteenth and nineteenth century that medicine made significant advances on epilepsy. Most of the advancements were made from religious believes. People thought that epilepsy was a divine punishment or possession from hell. In the beginning of the eighteenth century, it was a disease that only mentally ill people could have and therefore had a very low status in society; you were more likely to not receive any help from the state or medical care if you had epilepsy. In the late eighteenth century, important work was carried out by epileptologists William Culen (1710–1790) and Samuel A Tissot. They both studied the neurology of epilepsy and how epilepsy works. They correctly described the different types of epilepsy.

Focal or Partial Seizures

During these types of seizures, only half of the brain's hemisphere is affected by the seizure. The person is unconscious and loses sense of awareness in the attack of a seizure. As only one side is affected, they will still be able to remember what happened and communicate after the seizure is over.

General Seizures

These seizures are the most common types as they affect the whole brain. They are commonly known as:

Absence Seizures-This occurs when the person may faint or pass out without any convulsions (shaking). After the seizure, they will have no memory of it whatsoever. Absent seizures begin and end abruptly and without warning. This includes the person to stare which makes them look like they are day dreaming. They may even lose muscle control when the seizure is occurring. Absent seizures usually last up to ten seconds. And those getting seizures aren't confused; they can go back to normal activity once they feel they are ok.

Tonic-Clonic or Convulsive Seizures-These seizures make the patient lose consciousness immediately when the seizure starts. Usually, these seizures only last from one minute to three minutes but any longer than five minutes, there is a need to call an ambulance as you may require medical assistance. Clonic and tonic seizures have the same result in convulsions but different starts; with Clonic seizures most cases of patients experience muscle spasms or jerks as they are called which can be a key warning sign that you may have a seizure. When the spasms get worse, the patient may go into a full-blown seizure. The patient will lose consciousness throughout the duration of the seizure. Clonic seizures usually occur in early childhood. Bear in mind that clonic seizure can also appear at any age; in some cases teenagers going through puberty may get this type of seizure as the brain is changing so much during the course of puberty. My theory to this-when our bodies change physically, our brain has to adapt as well during puberty and our electrical messages work harder to meet the body's demands. Some cases the electrical messages can just get too much, so the brain releases the electrical messages via a seizure. This way the brain can reset and slow down. Teenagers can grow out of it in the end.

Tonic seizures are associated with another condition called multiple sclerosis (MS). These seizures start in early childhood although it can happen at any age. Tonic seizure has a lot of warning signs to bear in mind even though it's not as common as clonic seizures.

Atonic Seizures (drop seizures)

This is when a patient with no warning or sign falls onto the ground which can have a bad side effect of hurting themselves or bang their heads. It's very easy to get confused with this type of seizure and a faint. There are no convulsions when the seizure occurs; children tend to be more resilient than adults as when the seizure is over, they just continue with no worries at all. Adults tend to worry more but not in all cases.

Myclonic Seizures: The myclonic seizures come as a one off or a series. They include muscle jerks which happen on one side or the whole body is affected. A hand might suddenly jerk or a shoulder may suddenly raise up and your hips might move to one side abruptly, or your legs might kick out. Patients with this type may struggle to carry things like a cup of tea or coffee and the jerks makes their hands move so they spill it. Myclonic seizures starts in childhood but anybody at any age can suddenly get this type of epilepsy.

Additional Seizures

Infantile spasms-This type of epilepsy mainly occurs in babies. This type is very rare as epilepsy would normally occur in the early stages of childhood. This type starts from 3–7 months of the baby's life; the symptoms include-

Muscle spasms or quick movements.

The head may suddenly fall forwards.

The arms legs and the waist may flex cause them to be bend.

Each spasm usually lasts up to 1–2 seconds; it may seem longer as they come in a series of 5–50 spasms. They happen when the baby feels drowsy, or just about to go to sleep or woken up. This is because the brain activity changes between when we are tired and when we feel awake. Better source of electrical currents happens the more awake we are.

Psychogenic (Non-Epileptic Seizures)

These seizures are non-epileptic because the brain's electrical currents are normal, but the body still has convulsions. This can happen at any age but it's more common in 25–55-year-olds. Women are three times more likely to get this type then men are. It's caused by psychological changes in the brain through our thoughts. Stress may play a part in the cause but there's no certainty. It's so hard to tell the difference between these non-epileptic seizures and epileptic ones, so don't hesitate to record them so that a physiologist can look at it and notice any difference in the body's convulsions.

Is Epilepsy Genetic?

Well, the chances of epilepsy being genetic is very low even though it can be passed on through generations. But also, in some cases, even if your parents don't have epilepsy and it's not in the family tree, epilepsy can still occur later in life even if you haven't experienced it early in life as lifestyle can cause it.

In the beginning of the nineteenth century, new physicians started to come through with how society treated people with epilepsy. People started to understand the importance of getting them to hospital; while in hospital, epilepsy was categorised into two sections of the hospital, the insanity wards as neurological disorders were thought that people were insane by the condition at this time. and the sympathetic wards where doctors would just simply talk to patients and sympathise with them.

John Hughlings Jackson
4 April 1835–7 October
1911
Founder of Epilepsy

During the second half of the nineteenth century, new discoveries were being made after years of tests on the people who had epilepsy. French physicians came up with a new theory. Instead of epilepsy being caused by insanity, they had discovered that epilepsy was derived in the brain. This was proven as they studied long and hard on the mechanics of the brain. They conducted experiments on dogs by inducing electrical currents into the dog's brain which then caused electrical convulsions which gave the physicians the idea that epilepsy starts in the brain. John Hughlings Jackson (1835–1911) Father of Modern Epilepotology set the scientific base of epileptology as it was known in those days. His studies led him to the pathological and anatomical ways of epilepsy and in doing so, he discovered the name epilepsy as we know it today. John described the modern method of epilepsy as we know that patients have electrical convulsions in the brain. In his own words, he describing Epilepsy, 'Epilepsy is the name for occasional, sudden, excessive, rapid and local discharges of grey matter, which is the darker tissue that surrounds the brain and the spinal cord, which is mostly to do with the nerve cells in the tissue'.

History of Epileptic Medication

As far as therapies and the neurophysiology of epilepsy was concerned, much were already known during the second half of nineteenth century. Treatment of epilepsy consisted of herbal and chemical substances. In 1857, Sir Locock (1799–1875) discovered the anticonvulsant and sedative traits of potassium bromide. Also known as (KBR) as their chemical elements, this drug was also used to treat epilepsy in dogs; essentially this drug is a type of salt used as an anticonvulsant and a sedative to treat epilepsy in humans. This drug was a revolution as it was being taken by people on such a large scale that every single hospital had it at this time year. But it didn't come without its drawbacks; as it was a sedative, it became highly addictive. Often it would send people into illusion nightmares. There wasn't a better drug until the early twentieth century. In 1912, a new drug would take off called phenobarbital; this drug is still used today in developing countries as it's a cheap medicine to make. At this time it was not only used to treat epilepsy but was also used to treat difficulty sleeping, anxiety and drug withdrawal.

Phenobarbital was one of the very first epileptic drugs that was sold in the market or pharmaceuticals to patients. Dramatically more and more people were getting better. The success wasn't to last only a few years; later more and more people were complaining about the side effects of phenobarbital which was loss of breath, decreased level of consciousness; drastic action was taken as later on, it was found that people were still having seizures even after taking phenobarbital. This led to the introduction of animal testing to find other treatments. After 26 years of animal testing, there was a new drug on the market—Phenytoin in 1938, even though it was already known in 1908, there was no interest in using the drug but physicians at this time were adamant that there were anticonvulsant properties and had received good reviews in medical papers. So, phenytoin became the first medicine to prevent both partial and tonic-clonic seizures. This gave doctors alternative drugs to treat epilepsy. From 1946, we start to see another revolution in epilepsy medication as more and more drugs were appearing in the markets.

Trimethadione in 1946 used for absent seizures.

Carbamazepine in 1953.

Primidone in 1954.

Ethsuximide in 1958.

Sodium valproate in 1963.

Levitiracetam in 1992

Epilepsy Today

It's amazing how even today epilepsy has no real explanation in terms of causes or a cure. But there are many theories on what the cause of epilepsy could be. With medicine advancing every day, we will find a solution to cure epilepsy.

One final thing I'd like to leave this chapter with, it so happens to be a true story. One day I wanted to give blood, so in 2015, I think it was I went with my family to a blood bank which was in the local church. You go through all the process of filling the form out and having tests just to make sure you are eligible to give blood, so I got the tests done and unfortunately, I experienced epilepsy in my late teens because of this. They said, "I'm sorry to let you know but with your health history, we can't take the risk of taking your blood today," the head nurse said to me.

I was gutted because I wanted to help people by giving blood anyway, she went on to say that, "Knowing that you take a high dose of your medication, there is a risk that you could give someone epilepsy just through a blood transfusion." Now, I had a gut feeling that I wouldn't be able to give blood, but I never knew it would be that bad. In particular, I didn't know that I could give someone epilepsy just through blood. I just thought I'd mention it because it's a topic that simply doesn't get discussed and it's something that I think that needs to be talked about. I hope this doesn't put anyone off from giving blood; it's very important that we do it to saves lives. I just wanted to share my true story as it's another way we can get epilepsy.

Chapter XII
Multiple Sclerosis

The first recorded case of multiple sclerosis was in the early fourteenth century but not many people knew what to do at this time as medicine wasn't advanced then. MS was really difficult to treat and also very difficult to spot. MS is also very similar to motor neurone disease as they both affect the brain and the nervous system. The difference is that the immune system attacks the myelin sheath which acts like a shield that protects the nerves in the nervous system which debilitates the body over time; it's sometimes considered as an autoimmune disease. MS usually starts in early adulthood with age range of 20–40 years old. The symptoms of MS:

Fatigue.

Vision problems.

Mobility problems.

Depression/Anxiety.

Muscle spasms/stiffness/weakness.

Pain-neuropathic pain.

Speech and swallowing difficulties.

Numbness and tingling.

Luckily, most people only experience a few of these symptoms at the maximum. The severity of the symptoms depends on how bad the immune system damages the nerves as the messages that travel through the spinal cord and nerves slow down or get blocked. It's unclear how some patients don't experience any symptoms in the beginning, and some do. An idea of a mixture of genetics and environmental factors could be key. In a recent study, a new theory that T-cells also known as T lymphocyte are the cells that attack the myelin sheath. These T-cells are found in the thymus gland in the centre of the immune system. In the centre of the thymus gland is what's called the medulla and in there, thousands of T-cells are stored before they are assigned with their unique role. There are four types of T-cells:

Memory cells (protect us from viruses and tumours)

Regularity cells (modulates the immune system to maintain it against viruses and bacteria)

Killer cells (fights cancer)

Helper cells (send out signals to help regulate immune responses)

Who discovered MS? Well, this person is the same person who I've already talked about Motor Neurone Disease. He's **Charcot** French physician.

Jean was the first physician to find the symptoms of multiple sclerosis and also, he came up with the theory that it started from the nervous system. His method to explain it was by using the anatomy clinical method which is basically like an autopsy where he would look at patients that would have thought to have died from MS. He was able to look at the brain and the spinal cord and the immune system. He found that the myelin sheath which covers the nerves was severely damaged. He also came up with the theory that the motor system would be deeply affected and therefore, the reasons behind muscle stiffness/weakness would occur. This theory was proven right as it would be internationally recognised. He would then go on to teach the sign and symptoms of multiple sclerosis in lectures and he was the first person to diagnose MS on a living patient. Some of Jean's observations were so ahead of its time that it is only recently been recognised. One of them was the axonal transaction which basically describes the nerves sending through electric messages. If this ever gets damaged, then the motor system slowly loses its ability to move our muscles. Throughout the 1800s and early1900s. physicians were finding it hard to make any progress in treating MS. Deadly nightshade (a plant with poisonous fruit), arsenic, mercury, and the injection of malaria are just a few examples of the types of ineffective and even dangerous therapies that were once given to individuals with MS. In 1951, cortisone (steroid) was first used to treat MS relapses. Cortisone was found to reduce the severity of the relapse and to shorten its duration, but it had no long-term effects on the disease.

Types of Multiple Sclerosis

There are currently four types of MS that occurs:

Clinically isolated syndrome

This type of MS happens when the patient only experiences the symptoms of MS for 24hrs. If the symptoms persist longer, then doctors may diagnose you with the next type of MS.

Relapse-Remitting MS

This is the most common form of MS; it affects 85% of people that suffer with MS. The symptoms become more severe and keep on re-occurring. Even though symptoms worsen with this type, there is a good chance that the patient would be able to recover from the symptoms temporarily or even better, the symptoms would get better on their own.

Primarily Progressive MS

This type of MS symptoms are considerably worse without any warning signs or recovery time. Some patients may experience some stability with their symptoms while others may feel the symptoms will get worse before they can get better. Around 15% of people who have MS experience this type of condition.

Secondary Progressive MS

This type is similar to the primary one with the same symptoms, but the progressive nature of this type isn't as fast as the first one although the symptoms are still bad but don't progress as fast.

Is MS Genetic?

There is no clear evidence yet that MS is genetic because the gene hasn't yet been found but what is known is that MS is not inherited and it's not passed from parent to child.

MS Treatments

There is no cure for MS but there are treatments that can help with the symptoms:

Ways to help fatigue:

Exercise.

Keeping healthy sleep patterns.

Avoid medications that makes fatigue worse.

Be careful on caffeine use as it does help awaken you but when it wears off it can make you more fatigued after it wears off.

Muscle spasms/stiffness:

Regular routine of stretching will help.

If the muscle is more severe then you may be prescribed a medicine.

Physiotherapy.

Visual problems.

Sometimes visual impairment can improve within a few weeks

If symptoms are particularly severe, then you might be prescribed with steroids to speed up the process.

Mobility problems:

An exercise program supervised by a physiotherapist.

Vestibular rehabilitation for problems with balance.

Medication for dizziness or tremors.

Mobility aids such as a walking stick, or a wheelchair.

Home adaptations stair lifts or railings.

Neuropathic pain.

Medicines such as gabapentin or carbamazepine or amitriptyline.

Multiple Sclerosis Today

Today, scientists are looking into new treatments. Using stem cells to treat this condition is a ground breaking solution. They help regenerate brain cells which will make life so much easier as it will help slow down the progressive nature of the last two types of MS. But for now, we are relying on medications, therapies and exercise to help improve the way of life of MS even though we don't yet have a cure but at least we have something to look forward to.

Chapter XIII
Cystic Fibrosis

Throughout the ages of human history, loads of people were dying from Cystic Fibrosis; the first reference of the disorder was only a few centuries ago in European history. It was believed in the Middle Ages that a child with damaged pancreas and salt skin must die as the child was cursed. References of Cystic Fibrosis from old medical papers go back to the late 1500s; four centuries later in 1938, an American Pathologist Dr Dorothy Anderson provided the first description of the disease and even gave it a name 'Cystic Fibrosis of the pancreas' based on her research. She conducted autopsy on children that died from malnutrition. Other physicians of this time also named the condition as mucoviscidosis; this was named after thick mucus.

Dorothy along with her medical team managed to make the first ever tests to diagnose Cystic Fibrosis.

In modern history, there was a theory that a physicist found a genetic defect in a gene, but no one knew what the gene was and where it was in our chromosomes. At this time, it was just a theory that CF was caused by a gene defect. However, improvement in therapies and medicine made it possible to live a lot longer with the condition and help manage symptoms of CF which was the start of treating the condition. In 1948, Dr Paul di Sant 'Agnese observed infants that were dehydrated and he found infants that had CF had more concentration of salt in their sweat; so he validated that the old saying of the Middle Ages was right (not cursed). In 1980, the protein defect was detected and it wasn't until nine years later that they eventually found the gene that caused CF. This gene was called CTFR which had a mutation inside it. With new knowledge, new therapies were being created and medicines were being trialled which dramatically helped improve the survival rate for people with CF.

In recent years, public awareness about the condition skyrocketed. In the 1950s and 60s, new organisations were formed worldwide to help fundraising and other people with CF and so that families could meet up and feel normal in society. The CF foundation in America does an amazing job in raising awareness for CF providing research to discover new drugs and help spread more awareness to stop the stigma that goes around having CF.

Cystic Fibrosis Symptoms

Salty skin during sweating.
Persistent coughing with mucus.
Lung infections.
Difficulty breathing.
Wheezing shortness of breath.
Poor growth or weight gain.
Difficulty with bowel movements.
In some severe cases effects male infertility.

Treatments

Treatments differ in terms of the severity of the individual. Although many treatment plans have similar aspects that contain the same elements, but they are tailored to the individual's needs. Each day people with CF have to go through a number of different therapies.

Airways clearance-This helps loosen the muscles close to the lungs to help clear away and get rid of the thick mucus that builds up in the lungs.

Inhaled medicines-These are used to open the airways or thin the mucus. These are liquid medicines that are made into a mist or aerosol to fight lung infections and therapies to help keep airways clear.

Pancreatic Enzyme supplement-These are capsules that improve the absorption of vital nutrients. These are taken with every meal and most snacks. People with CF also usually take multivitamins.

Fitness plan-This helps improve energy, lung function, and overall health.

CFTR Modulators-These target the underlying defect in the CFTR protein. Because different mutations cause different defects in the protein, the medications that have been developed so far are effective, only with people with specific mutations.

The People Behind Cystic Fibrosis

Dr Dorothy Hansine Andersen (15 May 1901–3 March 1963) Founder of Cystic Fibrosis

Dr Dorothy Hansine Andersen was the first physician to identify cystic fibrosis as a disease and together with her research team, created the first tests to diagnose it. She also spent nearly a decade examining glycogen storage disease and studied cardiac malformations in great detail. She collected many specimens for her pathological research and left a valuable catalogue of disease used to pioneer new surgical treatments.

Dorothy was born in Asheville in North Carolina in 1901. Dorothy Andersen and her mother moved to Vermont after her Danish father died when she was 13. She attended Saint Johnsbury Academy and Mount Holyoke College. After earning her medical degree from Johns Hopkins University School of Medicine in 1926, Andersen completed a surgical internship at Strong Memorial Hospital in Rochester, New York; then taught anatomy at the University of Rochester. When she was denied a surgical residency at Strong Hospital because she was a woman, she joined the staff in the department of pathology at Columbia University College of Physicians and Surgeons. Between 1930 and 1935, while an instructor of pathology at Columbia, Andersen researched endocrine glands and female reproduction, also earning a doctorate of medical sciences in 1935.

That same year, she took up a position as assistant pathologist at a Babies Hospital at the Columbia-Presbyterian Medical Centre. Interested in inherited malformations of the heart, she began to collect the hearts of infants born with cardiac defects. In the mid-1940s, surgeons pioneering open-heart surgery sought out Andersen's help because of her vast knowledge of infant cardiology and her collection of specimens. She used her store of knowledge and experience to develop a training program for cardiac surgeons at several hospitals.

In 1958, she was made chief of pathology at Columbia-Presbyterian Hospital and a full professor of pathology at the Columbia University College of Physicians and Surgeons.

Andersen's duties included performing autopsies. While conducting an autopsy on a child who had presented the clinical picture of celiac disease an illness caused by an intestinal hypersensitivity to gluten that inhibits digestion, Andersen noticed a lesion in the pancreas. Following an extensive search of the autopsy records and related medical literature, she discovered a clear, though previously unrecognised, disease pattern. She called it cystic fibrosis. But Andersen did not think of herself solely as a pathologist and continued to work on diagnosing this new disease in living patients. Andersen and her research team made numerous discoveries that led to a simple diagnostic test for cystic fibrosis, one that is still in use today.

Dr Andersen considered herself a rugged individualist, a paediatric clinician, a research chemist, and a roofer and carpenter happy to make her own home improvements. Routinely described as 'windblown' by friends and detractors alike, she was considered quite a character. She is said to have kept a particularly untidy lab, holding semi-annual parties there, in honour of her Scandinavian heritage.

Dr Andersen was an honorary fellow of the American Academy of Paediatrics, and honorary chair of the National Cystic Fibrosis Research Foundation. She received numerous awards for her work, including the Elizabeth Blackwell Award in 1954 and the Distinguished Service Medal of the Columbia-Presbyterian Medical Centre in 1963.

Dr Paul di Sant'Agnese (1914–2005) Founder of Gene mutation for Cystic Fibrosis Founder of the Cystic Fibrosis Foundation

Cystic Fibrosis Today

People living with CF today have life expectancy that has been higher although some people might think that living for 37 years was too short. It used to be a lot shorter as people were dying in their late teens when research was first started. As therapies and treatments advance, life expectancy will improve as well. We certainly owe a lot to Dr Dorothy for her hard work in finding the first descriptions of the condition and Dr Paul for finally finding the gene. Cystic fibrosis is a crippling condition; however, there's always hope that we can continue the research of CF through their legacy to provide better care for patients with CF as science continues to advance.

Chapter XIV
Spina Bifida

Spina Bifida is a disability that dates back further to what we predicted in modern times just like osteogenesis imperfecta. Originally, we thought that spina bifida dated around the thirteenth century as physicians started researching it. It wasn't until we started doing research on Egyptian mummies that we discovered that spina bifida was around 12,000 BC. The cause of this condition could be that Egyptians believed in keeping the royal blood line pure, so by doing so they would breed with family members which would be with sisters, brothers, or cousins (which in those days was considered normal); it sadly led to have devastating consequences as a similar DNA pattern gave babies disabilities and miscarriages were common. A group of scientists recently discovered that there were two little children that were inside king Tutankhamen's tomb; these children were two daughters that were found to be his. The children were X-rayed and it was discovered that they also had a case of spina bifida which proved to be lethal as both daughters didn't live very long at all. They both tragically died at birth which would have been devastating for him and his wife.

Let's go forward to the future in around 400 BC; a well-known person lived around this time-Hippocrates. Hippocrates had a list of the disabilities that he documented; he was the first person to document spina bifida and treat it. It wasn't known as spina bifida at this time; it was known as hydrocephalus which means water in the brain similar to cerebral palsy. Hippocrates had a treatment plan to drill a hole inside the skull to drain out the liquid and fix the skull and you'd be fine. Sadly, there was another problem with this treatment; some patients at this time were complaining of brain damage which was a condition that Hippocrates thought that it would heal by itself, but it never did and therefore died from their injures. At the age of 90 years, he died and very little in terms of treatments was found to treat spinal bifida. Some physicians at this time tried at copying his techniques, but later found that the treatments weren't really working, so they went back to basics to try and figure out a new way.

In 160 AD, a Greek Physician called Galen who was quite popular in his day came up with the idea which involved twisting tree bark around the patient's head and inserting it into the hole after he drilled a hole into the skull similar to what Hippocrates did. Unsurprisingly, this treatment didn't work at all. In 650 AD, there was another physician called Paul of Aegina who came up with a theory that spina bifida was caused by midwives holding the baby's feet too hard during birth which again wasn't the cause.

Middle Ages

A new age approached and the medicine in the western world came to a halt as no one had an idea on further treatments for spina bifida but ideas came from the Middle East. Al-Zahrawi is considered to be one of the greatest surgeons in the Middle Age from the Islamic world. Not only he pioneered surgical procedures, but he also wrote a book of medical papers which was known as a medical encyclopaedia and was of 30 volumes. One of the problems he wrote about being treated was hydrocephalus. This is the first written description on treating spinal fluid. His thoughts of treating spina bifida were to use one of multiple incisions into the head which would've been better to drain the fluid as the hole would've been a lot smaller to drain, which also meant it would be less traumatic for the brain. In the sixteenth century when Elizabeth I was on the throne, people were intrigued with people with disabilities; so much so that they would write about them in their journals or put them in the newspapers at the time. Not all news was positive as it made them look like freak shows. But the positive side of this was that it got people talking about disability, and led to more awareness, particularly for Spina Bifida at this time.

Nicholas Tulp 9 October 1593– 12 September 1674

Founder of the name Spina Bifida

Nearly 100 years later in 1685, Dutch surgeon Nicolas Tulp was the first person to use the term spina bifida whilst writing about it in his medical papers. On one occasion, he treated a young boy who had the condition; he had the idea of puncturing the sac on his lower back; unfortunately the young boy died after the treatment. But it wasn't a death in vain as he later discovered an element in the sac which would be crucial in treating spina bifida in the future. In 1761, Giovanni Battista Morgagni was the first person to fully describe the symptoms of hydrocephalus, and made a clear connection between spina bifida and hydrocephalus. He mentioned that people can get spina bifida with or without hydrocephalus.

In 1875, Rudolf Ludwig Carl Virchow commonly known as the 'pope of medicine' amongst his colleagues was the first person to describe and start using the term 'spina bifida occulta'. In 1892, it was reported that German surgeon C Bayer performed the first surgery repair on an open myelomeningocele, which is the birth defect of the spinal fluid and doesn't allow the spinal canal to close before birth. This is the most common form of spina bifida. He used an innovative method of a series of rotating flap techniques with moderate success. It was considered a remarkable advance and was sure to be adopted by many other surgeons of this time.

Throughout the nineteenth century, more and more surgeons were attempting a similar surgery as C Bayer but had very little success; many patients died. One of the main causes was the aftercare like infections or septicaemia. Surgeries changed again as new surgical techniques were developed. In the 1860s, when patients had hydrocephalus, Dr James Morton had the idea to stick needles through the swollen sac and inject iodine and glycerine solution to drain out the liquid which was successful at the time and surgeons still use iodine today to keep the wound clean before and after surgery. Iodine is still used today not only for spinal bifida but before all surgeries as they play a vital role in keeping everything clean and hygienic. This was the start for people to not only have surgery but survive after it as infections were rife at this time as these were very difficult to control but iodine kept these under control. While patients with myelomeningocele were vastly improving, there was another type of spina bifida which was still killing people because there wasn't anything good enough to treat them.

In the 1950s, many people with Hydrocephalus (liquid on the brain) still had a very high death rate. In 1955, there was a little boy called Casey who was born in Connecticut in America. Casey was born with liquid on the brain similar to cerebral palsy, but the difference is cerebral palsy is genetic whereas hydrocephalus is caused by a haemorrhage, an infection similar to meningitis, trauma during delivery or after birth. Back to Casey, his doctor called Dr Holter worked day and night to try and invent a device that could be slotted into the brain and drain the excess liquid. Dr Holter then met another doctor called Dr Spitz; they both worked together and eventually came up with a device which was named after them the Holter-Spitz shut or valve. But unfortunately, it was too late to save Casey and he died by the time the valve was ready. But his death wasn't in vain as his dad made sure that this valve would be known and promoted to other families with similar circumstances. Casey's father managed to help save millions of lives in the process. At this point, spina bifida as a whole took a massive turn for the better as the death rate was massively declining. But the success wasn't to last long as 20 years later, the valve needed constant revision and the long-term effects of having this valve was impacting the bladder which then led to kidney failure which was another cause of death. Throughout the 70s and 80s as cases were treated on a case-by-case basis if the symptoms of spina bifida were obvious; the doctors would perform the surgery of removing the sac away but if the symptoms weren't so obvious. then some patients would be waiting up to two years before any treatments.

From 1955 to 1962, a team of doctors analysed 522 cases of spina bifida and with the results came to an agreement that they had no facility for the selection of patients that needed traditional treatments rather than surgical treatments on the grounds of paralysis, deformity, hydrocephalus at birth. This led to most centres in the United Kingdom and United States to adopt the idea of performing surgeries within 12–48 hours after birth. However, Dr John Lorber had different ideas; his opinions were that disabled infants had very few or no friends and most of the time were left without jobs and were unable to live in society as they couldn't live the same as able-bodied people. To make matters worse, he came up with his own medical criteria. Patients that didn't meet the needs of his rules would go without food and drink and antibiotics for treatment; this was a very strict rule which led to most patients not even meeting his cruel criteria. Unfortunately, Dr Lorber's criteria was adopted throughout the 70s and 80s.

Later on, most of the doctors were unhappy with the progress that Dr Lorber was making, so they rejected his criteria and allowed food and antibiotics to be allowed for everyone. Towards the end of the 1980s, there were better valve designs and better bladder treatments. Patients were having fewer complaints but the debate between Dr Lorber and the medical practice was still on.

Treating spina bifida today still makes use of similar surgeries as it was in the 80s within 48hrs of birth. Surgeons perform surgery to remove the excess liquid in the sac at the bottom of the spine and repair the spinal canal. After surgery, every baby is closely monitored. With hydrocephalus, a small thin tube is used and this is implanted into a thin soft pallet of the brain and drains the excess fluid and transfers it to another part of the body usually the stomach. The patient may need to use a shunt all of their lives as the liquid may always reappear. They may need a different shunt throughout their life as the shunt might get too small as the child gets older or the shunt might get infected or blocked and will need urgent replacement.

What Is Spina Bifida?

First thing to know is that there are three main types of spina bifida. The first type is called occulta which is the least severe case and fortunately the most common. It is really hard to see the changes in the lower spine as the spine appears to be the closest to normal looking; the only difference is that there's a very small lump in the lower part of the spine which isn't lethal but needs to be removed as it only affects the area of the skin. Most people don't even know if they have it as it can only be detected in an X-ray or a scan.

The second type is called meningocele where you can see that there is a sack of liquid opening the lower part of the spine. It is not as big as the third type. This is caused by a birth defect which grows into a sac full of liquid which also contains membranes that cover the central nervous system. It is considered to be a neural tube defect with the rarest form of spina bifida. The odds of getting this type is 1 to 1000 births, which brings us to the third and final type of spina bifida which is called myelomeningocele. This is the worst type of spina bifida; it is a malformation of the closure of the spinal cord closing in the lower back region when the backbone and the spinal canal can't close while growing in the womb. As spina bifida is a progressive condition, over time the spinal cord will experience damage and so a surgery is needed to remove the sac and close the backbone into the spinal cord and stitch the skin back together. However, surgery can't cure nerve damage; once that is damaged then the patient will have to find ways to get help later in life depending on how bad the damage is. Another part of myelomeningocele is babies will experience liquid inside the brain similar to cerebral palsy which is called hydrocephalus. It cannot only damage the brain but also damage brain development. They treat this by making a silicone shunt (valve) placing it through a hole in the back of the head into the brain. The liquid gets transported through the tube and down into the stomach so that the body can get rid of it naturally. It's not a cure but it helps control the symptoms, but it makes a huge difference in saving lives. The shunt needs to be looked after because over time, the infection can get inside the tube which will need replacing in order to keep working. There also other side effects that come with myelomeningocele such as:

Bladder and bowel problems.

Breathing problems.

Tube in the stomach to eat.

Club feet due to lack of formation to the feet and ankles.

Curvature to the spine.

These extra side effects will continue into adulthood, so make sure that you attend regular GP appointments and you should be ok.

The People Behind Spina Bifida Rudolf was a pathologist and a politician and was regarded as one of the greatest pathologists in history because he was the first physician to identify diseases with malfunctioning cells.

Rudolf was born on 13 October 1821 in Poland but at this time, Germany had taken power over Poland, so it was called Schievelbein, but now Poland is an independent country and renamed Świdwin. His father Carl Christian Siegeed Virchow was a farmer and town treasurer of Schievelbein. His mother was Johanna Maria Hesse. The couple weren't particularly rich and Rudolf was their only child. His parents loved the natural world and passed the love onto Rudolf, taking him on bird watching trips. Rudolf attended the local primary school in Schivelbein. From his early days at school, he seemed to be exceptionally gifted intellectually, so much so that his parents paid for extra lessons to push him even more. Rudolf later on professed to an academic school which was in Köslin-a school for very strong students. Rudolf's secondary school curriculum was classical learning Greek and Latin which wasn't a problem for him as he had a talent for learning languages, he also learnt Dutch, English, French and Hebrew in his spare time. Between school and medical school he taught himself Italian which meant he could speak eight languages. In 1839, at the age of 17, he graduated from secondary school. He won a scholarship which led him to go and study medicine at the Friedrich-Wilhelms University in Berlin, Prussia's capital city. He completed his course at the age of 21; he worked in a number of medical jobs but one of his passions was pathology-the study of disease. In his earliest work, he studied a lot on cells and

Rudolf Ludwig Carl Virchow 13 October 1821– 15 September 1902 Founder of Spina Bifida

what their roles were and what caused them to change in the event of mutated cells. Rudolf was the first to carry out autopsies that involved microscopic examination. In 1845, he published his first paper in science. In the paper, he published his writings that were the first findings of leukaemia; he described the name by combining two Greek words leukos (white) and aima (blood).

Rudolf used his autoptic skills to cut into a young infant's lower back and into the sac from which the liquid came out and underneath was the spinal cord which looked anything but healthy. During this time, the condition had no name; eventually, Rudolf came up with the name spina bifida as we know today. He wrote the name down in his medical papers; he came up with the theory that spina bifida maybe caused by a germ and many physicians at this time believed it was true. Later on, it was discovered that it was no longer the case. Not only did Rudolph find the name for spina bifida but he also founded other conditions such as parenchyma, vertebral disc rupture. Throughout his career, Rudolph had theories that were found correct and also found wrong. For example, he had an idea that cancer was caused by cells which is true but then went onto the idea that it was also caused by tissue irritation which was later to discovered to be wrong. However, Rudolph found the beginnings for treating cancer as cancer cells were later discovered.

Other Careers

Despite Rudolph excelling in medical science, he also had different hobbies as an anthropologist and a politician. He certainly put these into good use as this was a time of severe poverty and disease. There wasn't enough clean water to go around and food for the poor. He worked to build a better sewage system so that hygiene standards could improve. Virchow had very liberal views, believed in good education, living conditions and better health conditions for the poor. He knew by being hygienic, cells that caused disease could be killed and this could save the lives of many.

Later Years

In the last decade of his life, Rudolph and his three sons travelled to the northern coast of Germany where they found an island. He and his sons found a house where he co-founded the German Anthropological Association and the Society for Anthropology.

In 1902, at the age of 80, he fell off a tram car and fractured his femur. However, it wasn't the cause of his death as many thought. In the process of his femur getting better, he suffered a heart attack and died leaving a loving wife and three sons and three daughters behind.

Rudolph Virchow's Legacy

He was the first physician to discover autopsy.

First to name spina bifida and others.

First to discover leukaemia.

Through his fascination of microscopic cells, he discovered that cells could be mutated to form disability.

Awards

In 1892, Rudolph was awarded the highest prize in science of his time-the British Royal Society's Copley Medal for his services to medical science.

Dr James Morton was born in Glasgow, Scotland in 1820 at the age of 21. Morton studied medicine at Anderson's University for three years but then moved to Edinburgh in 1844 at the age of 24. A year later, he graduated and got his medical degree and moved back to Glasgow in 1845 where he settled in 1851 and became a fellow of the FPSG. Morton later became a professor of material medical at Anderson's University and at Anderson's College of Medicine from 1855 until 1888; he worked as a surgeon at the Glasgow Royal Infirmary from (1859–1867) and (1870–1885). Morton led a host of Glasgow surgeons who sought to ridicule Lister's work on antisepsis during the 1860s and 1870s and he attempted to debunk Louis Pasteur's germ theory. History has judged him kindlier for developing an antiseptic injection, treatment for spina bifida which was later endorsed by a special committee of the clinical society of London. He received many honours for his work as he was elected president of the west Scottish branch of British Medical Association. In 1886, he was elected president of the faculty of physicians and surgeons of Glasgow and became a long-time member of the examining board. He was re-elected for two straight years, was awarded the British Medical Association in 1888 in Kibble

Dr James Morton (1820–1889) Founder of the Antiseptic Injection

Palace. Dr James always approached his work with high standards which would always pay well for him as he made very few enemies. During his later years, he mellowed, and his character was softer.

Dr James Morton's Legacy

James's work was incredible in finding that Iodine glycerine injection helped save many babies with spina bifida as surgeons could operate without fear of the patient getting infected as time once told.

Spina Bifida Today

In America, the statistics show that infants that are born with spina bifida come to 1–2 in 1,000 but research in 1998 has shown that folic acid can dramatically decrease the odds of getting spina bifida by 70%. Folic acid also decreases the defects of spina bifida in general. The most common form of spina bifida is myelomeningocele, which affects around 1,500 babies each year. The average case for spina bifida worldwide is 1 in 1,000 babies. The percentage taken form 10,000 births, we found that there was 0.9 percent in Canada, 0.7 percent in France to 7.7 percent in United Arab Emirates. In South America, it is 11.7 percent. One of the highest statistics is in Britain, particularly in Wales and Ireland with 3–4 out of 1,000 babies having spina bifida compared to countries like France, Japan, Norway, Hungary, Czechoslovakia and Yugoslavia where only 0.1–0.6 cases per 1,000 births occur which is absolutely astounding. These numbers need to be looked at as a guide to see what needs to be done to help bring the numbers down. One day, I think we will with advanced medicine and fiction will turn to reality.

Chapter XV
Muscular Dystrophy

Unfortunately, there wasn't a census that was written to suggest that muscular dystrophy was around in the ancient Egyptian times or the ancient Roman times etc. It wasn't until the nineteenth century when muscular dystrophy was first mentioned by Sir Charles Bell (1774–1842). In 1830, he wrote about a mysterious illness of this time. He may not have come up with a name for it but he knew that this illness was progressive and worsened over time in young boys. In 1836, there was another document that was written by two physicians Giovanni Semmola's and Gaetano Conte; they wrote about a family with two young brothers who had a progressive muscle weakness. In 1852, Dr Edward Meryon (1809–1880) described a family with four boys, all experiencing the same muscle weakness as the two brothers did. This story caught attention by one physician in particular, French neurologist Guillaume Benjamin Duchenne. (1806–1875). He wrote the first case of muscular dystrophy in 1861 where the muscles get weaker and weaker over time. In 1868, he gave an account of 13 patients with muscular dystrophy. One of the most severe and well-known case of the condition is what he named after himself which is Duchenne Muscular Dystrophy. Now, there's at least nine different types of MD.

Myotonic

This is the most common type of MD in adults. Mytonic MD can affect both men and women; only in rare cases would you expect a new born to experience this type known as congenital MMD. Mytonic comes from prolonged spasms or stiffening of the muscles. The disorder causes muscle to weaken and also affects the central nervous system, heart, stomach, eyes, hormone producing glands. In most cases, daily living isn't restricted as some people may think. However, life expectancy is decreased.

Duchenne

This type is the most common of muscular dystrophy in young children. It affects only young boys and starts between the ages between 2 and 6. The muscles decrease in size and grow weaker over time yet may appear larger. The progression of the disorder can vary but many people with Duchenne (1 in 3,500 boys) need a wheelchair by the age of 12. In most cases, the arms and legs and spine may become deformed as the muscles around aren't strong enough to support and maintain its structure. Cognitive and impairment issues may occur. Severe breathing and heart problems mark the later stages of the disorder. Those with Duchenne MD usually die in their late teens or early 20s due to the severity of this type of MD.

Becker

This form is similar to Duchenne muscular dystrophy, but the disorder is more forgiving. Symptoms appear later and progress is a lot slower. It usually appears between the ages of 2 and 16 but can appear as late as age of 25. Like Duchenne, Becker MD affects only boys (1 in 30,000). Becker MD can also cause heart problems. Again, severity still varies from person to person. People with Becker MD can walk until their 30s and live older through adulthood.

Limb-Girdle

This type appears to be more common in teenagers and young adults and can affect both men and women. In its most common form, limb girdle MD causes progressive weakness that begins in the hips and moves to the shoulders, arms, and legs. Within 20 years, walking becomes more difficult over time and later on, one may need a wheelchair. Sufferers may live to their 40s or late 70s.

Facioscapulohumeral

This type refers to the muscles that move in the face, shoulder blade, and upper arm bone. This form of MD appears in teenagers or in early adulthood and affects men and women. It progresses slowly, with short periods of rapid muscle deterioration and weakness. Severity ranges from very mild to completely disabling. Walking, chewing, swallowing, and speaking problems can occur. About 50% of those with Facioscapulohumeral MD can walk throughout their lives, and also people with this condition have a normal life span.

Congenital

This type is present at birth. Congenital MD progresses slowly in men and women. Myosin deficiency can cause muscle weakness at birth or a little afterwards along with severe contractions (shortening or shrinking of muscles) which can cause joint problems later in life. Patients may also expect to experience abnormalities which may include differences in the brain and also seizures.

Oculopharyngeal

This type affects the eyes and the throat and can affect both men and women, between their 40s and 60s. Again this type progresses slowly causing weakness in the eyes and face muscles which may make it harder to swallow. Patients may experience weakness in the pelvis and shoulder muscles which normally occurs later in life. Choking and pneumonia may also occur which is due to the weak muscles surging the throat and lungs.

Distal

This is a rare form of MD. Distal affects both men and women; it causes muscle wastage in the distal muscles which are located in the forearms, hands, lower legs and feet. It is generally less severe and progresses slower than other types of MD and affects fewer muscles which often leaves it harder to diagnose as it is a rare form.

Emery-Dreifuss

This is another rare form of MD. This type appears from childhood to teenage years. It affects mainly boys, but girls can get it but it is less common for that to happen. It causes muscle weakness in the shoulders, upper arms, lower legs. Emery-Dreifuss is more life threatening as heart problems can occur. Muscle weakness can also spread to the chest and pelvic muscles. One positive thing is that the muscle weakness is less severe than other types of MD and patients need to monitor the heart with regular checks.

What Is Muscular Dystrophy?

Originally known as Duchenne Muscular Dystrophy, it is a rapid progressive form of MD that occurs only in boys and it is caused by a gene mutation called the DMD gene that is in the X chromosome. It is inherited from families who have it from previous family members or it can just happen without any family history of having the condition. Patients who have the condition will have progressive muscle loss, function and weakness, which begins in the lower limbs. The DMD gene is the second largest in the X chromosome which encodes the muscle protein (dystrophin). Boys with DMD don't make the dystrophin protein in their muscles which helps maintains muscle fibres. The symptoms usually start between infancy and 6 years of age. The most noticeable symptom is a delay in motor milestones in walking, talking, sitting and standing. The main age for walking with DMD is 18 months; however, the progressive muscle weakness in the lower limbs and the pelvic muscles can cause waddling difficultly climbing stairs. Muscle weakness can occur in the upper body as well it is not as severe as the lower body affecting the arms, neck and other areas. Calf muscles become enlarged which is treated by replacing the muscle with fat and connective tissue (Pseudohypertrophy). Muscle contractions happen in the legs making them unusable because the muscle fibres are shortened and fibrosis occurs in the connective tissue. Occasionally, it can cause pain. Between the age of 6 and 11, the decline of muscle strength starts at the age of 10; leg braces are used to try and maintain some strength in the legs but by the age of 12, most boys are confined to a wheelchair. Bones can develop abnormally causing skeletal deformities of the spine, pelvic area and other areas.

Where Is the Gene Located?

The mutated gene is in the X chromosome; it is the second largest gene in our chromosomes and it is located between XP21.1 and XP21.2. This gene is responsible for encoding dystrophin which helps muscles last. As the gene is mutated, patients with Duchenne have no dystrophin at all and so they have a shorter life compared to Becker MD patients and so they can live longer or close to a normal life.

Who Discovered Muscular Dystrophy?

Guillaume Benjamin Duchenne
(17 September 1806–15 September 1875)
Founder of Neurology
Founder of Muscular Dystrophy

Guillaume was born in Paris, France on the 17 September 1806. He was the son of a fisherman, to which his father had a long line of fishermen in his family and naturally his father wanted him to follow in his footsteps to which he said no. Going against his father's wishes, Guillaume was interested in science from a young age to which he enrolled at the University of Duai in France. He managed to get a bachelor's degree at the age of 19. He was trained by the best physicians of this time, before returning to Boulogne and set up his own practice there. Duchenne soon after met a woman he loved and got married and they had a baby boy but sadly his wife passed away whilst giving birth which was heart-breaking for him. Whilst his son was growing up, they both didn't get on at all, even though his son like his father, got into the medical industry. Despite difficult times, they began to see eye to eye later on in Duchenne's life. In 1835, Duchenne began to experiment with what was known as 'electropuncture' which had been recently invented by physicians François Magendie and Jean-Baptiste Sarlandière using electric shocks were administrated beneath the skin with sharp electrodes to stimulate the muscles. Duchenne got married again but it was only brief as it didn't last and ended up in divorce but he stayed in Paris to further his research; he didn't achieve any senior roles in the medical practice but he did support himself by creating his own small private medical practice and at the same time attended different hospitals that would teach other physicians neurology. He developed a non-invasive way of stimulating muscles by shocking the surface of the skin which he called 'electrisation localisèe'. He published them in his medical papers in 1855 and in 1862, he published the same work but with pictures; a few months later, he published a book which is the start of the discovery of muscular dystrophy which is called the *Mechanism of Human Physiognomy*. To cut a long story short, it's about a case where Duchenne discovered a young boy had what he called Duchenne Muscular Dystrophy which we know is the most severe case of the condition. A year later, he also provided pictures of the boy in a photo album that he published. Later on, he provided 13 more children cases with muscular dystrophy. He was the first physician of his time to do a biopsy while they were alive to obtain muscle tissue for microscopic examination.

Legacy

One of the first physicians of his time who learnt how neurological pathways worked in the brain and then later on, he developed a way of doing a biopsy for muscle examination which led to the discovery of muscular dystrophy. One bonus fact about Guillaume is that when he was a teacher, he taught one of the greatest physicians we have ever had-Jean-Martin Charcot who we all know went on to do great things. Jean once quoted about him saying, 'my teacher in neurology'. Before Guillaume, neurology didn't even exist, so with his knowledge, he taught younger physicians the different mechanics of the brain. Quite remarkable.

Muscular Dystrophy Today

Today, Muscular Dystrophy mainly affects mainly affects men as women have two X chromosomes and no Y chromosome as having 2 X chromosomes proves stronger in fighting the symptoms of MD. However, this doesn't mean that women aren't completely immune to MD because if it was a Duchenne gene mutation, then there is a chance that a girl will get MD but this is incredibly rare; only 8% of patients of MD are girls; the rest are boys. Also as women have 2 X chromosomes, if one chromosome is affected with the Duchenne gene then there is a backup which leads women to be carriers whereas men aren't so lucky as they have a copy of the Y chromosome as there is only one copy of the X chromosome; this leads men to develop symptoms of MD later in life.

Chapter XVI
Tourette's Syndrome

Tourette's has a longer history than people may think. The earliest mention of the condition goes back to the fifteenth century where an author called Jakob Sprenger and Heinrich Kraemer wrote a book called *Malleus Malificarum* which means (Witches Hammer). In this story is described a priest who had been suffering with tick which were thought to be related to the possession of the devil. In the nineteenth century, neurology was at the peak of its revolution ever since Jean-Martin Charcot set the foundations for neurology; his teachings inspired a generation of new neurologists. New mental disorders were being diagnosed throughout this century and a new neurologist from France would describe the first symptoms of Tourette's. Towards the late nineteenth century, very little progress was being made in terms of treatment and causes of ticks. With limited knowledge, they only had ideas, which included brain lesions similar to rheumatic chorea which explains the muscle movements in the head and face. The movements can also happen in the feet which is caused by faulty motor movements. Physician Sigmund Freud had developed psychoanalysis to treat the ticks which had some success as it was carried on to the twentieth Century.

In the beginning of the twentieth century, there was an idea that Tourette's came from an organic origin meaning that a patient would have a disease that changed the body and mind to cause the ticks similar to a disease with side effects; physicians believed this for quite some time. Then in the 1930s, physicians thought that there were more causes then that. Some physicians thought that psychiatric problems or traumas could be the cause of the ticks. Then in the 1970s, Sigmund's psychoanalysis was re-used to treat the condition. In 1958, there was a new drug that hit the medical practice called haloperidol. Originally made to treat schizophrenia and other psychotic symptoms, this was also given to patients to help ease the ticks. This drug was founded by a pharmacist called Paul Janssen.

Haloperidol was developed to block the effects of dopamine, which effects thoughts and feelings. Later on, the drug entered its first clinical trials, then nine years later, it was approved by America. In the early nineteenth century, Tourette's was seen by physicians as a psychotic brain disease whereby certain thoughts or behaviours caused the ticks to occur. As the new drug was in place for patients to take, Sigmund Freud's treatment of psychoanalytic treatments for Tourette syndrome were questioned. The first description of haloperidol in the treatment of Tourette's was published by Seignot in 1961 which in itself was a breakthrough because treatment became instant. In 1965, Arthur K Shapiro described as the father of modern tick disorder treated a Tourette's patient with haloperidol. Dr Shapiro and his wife, Elaine Shapiro who had a PhD herself reported the treatment in a 1968 article, and severely criticised Sigmund's psychoanalytic approach.

The Shapiros working with the patient's families found in 1972 the Tourette Syndrome Association (TSA later renamed to Tourette Association of America in 2015). Thanks to the association, they had discovered that Tourette's was no longer a psychotic disease but neurological disorder which made doctors argue about it. However, the media played a key role in spreading awareness for neurological disorders which helped the argument. The original case reports of TS were by French neurologists, the focus moved to New York in the 1970s and the centre for the most committed progress in TS continued in the USA; thanks to the Tourette Syndrome Association.

Tourette's Syndrome Today

Tourette's affects different parts of the brain, including an area called the basal ganglia which helps body movements. Any differences in basal ganglia may affect nerve cells and the chemicals that carry messages between the brain and the body. New research has shown that the brain's network plays a role. Doctors don't yet know the true cause of Tourette's, but a new study is showing that our genes could be a cause. People who have Tourette's in the family are most likely to get it. However, there is a difference in terms of how bad the symptoms will be. Another cause of Tourette's could be autistic spectrum, because epilepsy is linked to the spectrum. The brain's electrical currents could react similarly in the network as epilepsy for Tourette's.

George was born in France on 30 October 1857 in a small town called Saint-Gervais-les-Trois-Clochers in the county of Châtellerault, near the city of Loudun. In his day, he would be respectfully known neurologist, but the field did not exist in his time. Just at the tender age of 16, George first started his medical studies at Poitiers. He later on moved to Paris where he became a student, a secretary or personal assistant and a house physician. One of his mentors was a neurologist I've already talked about-Jean-Martin Charcot. Jean played a key role in the development in George's academic career in teaching him the fundamentals of modern neurology; just a few years later, George had his own lectures in psychotherapy, and modern-day hypnosis. At the age of 27, George started describing the first symptoms of Tourette's He learned about a condition where people were experiencing verbal ticks. Many people who suffered with this condition got very frustrated that they had no control of it. Hence, people thought in the fifteenth century, it was from the devil.

He researched nine people who had Tourette's syndrome, but he didn't call it Tourette's straightaway instead he came up with a different name called 'maladie deistic'. George was one of Jean-Martin Charcot's favourite students, so he renamed what George had found in his research and named it after him in his honour Tourette's Syndrome.

In 1893, one of George's patients who had suffered with Tourette's Syndrome shot George in the head as she believed that George had caused her to have Tourette's through hypnosis. Hypnosis was a treatment that George came up with, but it had mixed results. Later on, in the same year, came more bad news for George as one of his best friends and mentor Jean-Martin Charcot died; to top it off, he lost his young son. After these events, George began to have mood swings and depression. But he didn't let it hold him back as he continued giving lectures of literacy, mesmerism and theatre. In 1902, George's mental health continued to worsen, so he was dismissed from his post. On 26 May 1904, in a psychiatric hospital, he died at the age of 46.

Arthur K Shapiro was born in Brooklyn, New York; in 1951, he graduated from City College of New York where he obtained his medical degree. In 1955, he went to the University of Chicago where he was the director of the special studies in laboratory at Cornell University until 1977; later, he became a physician at Mount Sinai School of Medicine in Manhattan.

Arthur had a big collection of medical antiques. Arthur and his wife Elaine were married for 46 years; they were so devoted to each other that they didn't even let work get in the way of their pioneering research with Tourette's. After Arthur died of lung cancer at the age of 72, Elaine helped finish the last book that they both wrote called *The Powerful Placebo-from ancient priest to modern physician.*

Legacy

Arthur and Elaine Shapiro had achieved so much in bringing a shift in what physicians previously thought that Tourette's was psychotic to neurological and changing the way that we treat it through medicine rather than therapy.

Tourette's Today

Tourette's is seen as the talking condition but it is hard to control but we are making small steps to making a difference as doctors know which part of the brain called the basal ganglia which is the area of the brain which is responsible for movement and Tourette's Syndrome. In recent years, there's been a debate on whether Tourette's would be on the autism spectrum along with epilepsy as in the beginning, doctors thought that autism and Tourette's were completely different things. But then soon after more information came from studies that doctors had done on autism, they found that epilepsy was on the autism spectrum along with ADHD and Asperger's Syndrome. As epilepsy was a close cousin to Tourette's, they decided to add it to the spectrum as well. There are other things that a patient would experience with Tourette's which is OCD and anxiety. In OCD, people follow certain rituals or behaviours in order to help the ticks as the rituals provide a bit of relief for the individual and as for anxiety, if the patient feels stressed, this could make the ticks worse, therefore ways to relax to keep calm for the ticks to improve were needed. There are always ideas that could be tried to treat Tourette's as I believe that even the brain can have problems but it can also treat itself by the placebo effect or meditation or even stem cells that can be used to try and repair the way that the brain is wired, so that the brain won't suffer from Tourette's anymore. At the moment, Tourette's is mainly treated by anti-epileptic drugs due to the ticks which don't always work as everyone reacts differently to drugs. One day, we will find the cure for Tourette's as research will advance to try out new ideas. Soon, it won't be seen as a hopeless condition to treat.

Chapter XVII
Deaf

Deaf people have pretty much been around since when humans and animals roamed the earth. Even if they didn't have serious symptoms of hearing loss, due to lack of hygiene, there would have been ear wax blocking their ears. It is in ancient Egypt where you'll find the first-ever recording of deaf people. The Ebers Papyrus which dates back to around 1550 BC which is the oldest medical document in the world would have a list of different diseases and gives some remedies which the Egyptians believed to have worked. For deaf people, there was only a certain number of things that they could do. What they thought of doing was to put olive oil, red lead, ant eggs, bag wings, and goat urine into the ears to help temporary hearing. The olive oil might help the ear wax but may not work on serious deafness. There wasn't any stigma or bad experiences for dead people as the Egyptians believed that disabled people were closer to God, so they treated deaf people with kindness. In Ancient Greece, attitudes towards disabled people were different.

Around 350 BC, Greek physicians Aristotle and Plato thought that people who were born deaf would end up being unintelligent; this started the stigma that stayed throughout human history for centuries. Across Europe, millions of disabled people didn't get help that they needed simply because of this belief. Despite the stigma, Plato was the first person to reference sign language by thinking if people had no voice or tongue, there would be another way to communicate through hand gestures, body language, reading lip movements etc. Plato's first reference wasn't well known at this time, so many deaf people were still getting by without the ability to communicate properly; this went on for centuries until the tenth century where the first attempts for sign language were from monks.

In Burgundy, France, monks taught a series of hand gestures to deaf people which would later turn out to be the beginning of sign language. Also, monks used this way of communication to talk to one another while being quiet during prayer.

The first form of sign language was called Cluniac sign language. The first sign language that was ever used originally founded by monks was Cluniac sign language and was used to spell each letter which would then lead to making words and sentences etc. This gave deaf people the power of communication for the first time. With this skill, they could communicate with both deaf and able people which opened up their world. The first mention of the hearing aid dates back to the ancient Roman times where the idea of using animal horns to make a telescope to fit around the ear was used to allow people to hear better; this idea didn't come into use until quite late in the fifteenth century. With the written evidence of hearing aids and sign language, this helped stop the stigma away for deaf people by the end of the sixteenth century, which leads to the next question were there any other causes other than conductive hear loss that would cause deafness?

Well, an ancient mummy called Pum II had a burst ear drum as archaeologists dug up his body. However, no one knows how his ear drum burst but one suggestion says that the bones around the ear drum were too small to give the ear drum room to hear and so the ear just collapsed. This is what happens sometimes when patients have brittle bones. The earliest prediction of this happening would suggest that this occurred 10,000 years ago. Another cave had other mummies inside; when archaeologists dug up their corpses, some had a part of a bone that was growing inside the ear canal which would affect hearing as well.

Archaeologists have done some more research and some of the skeletons may not even be our human skeleton but a different type of skeleton altogether known as the Neanderthals. If this is true, then deafness has a longer history than previously known. If the research is correct, then deafness would go back between 30,000 years to 350,000 years when the Neanderthals ruled Europe. We know this because a team of archaeologists found a good number of skeletons belonging to the Neanderthals. The Neanderthals were a lot broader and bigger than modern humans. They even used tools like our ancestors did which would suggest that they were intelligent like us as well, but they may not have known the importance of cleaning out the ears as the ear wax would block the ear canal forcing deafness. You're probably thinking how did it pass on from the Neanderthals to modern humans? Well, 40,000 years ago, the Neanderthals mated with modern humans which led to their genes being passed to us. congenital deafness is a genetic mutation passed on, so maybe it started from the

Neanderthals, but of course, environmental deafness can be prevented through good hygiene and avoiding extremely loud noises. In order to figure out what living with deafness was like in the past, it is the best to look into history of education as it affects us all and society.

Deaf Education History

Deafness through the centuries has come a long way. At the very beginning of Ancient Greece in the eighth century, people believed that deaf people weren't intelligent, so they weren't suitable for an education. This didn't just happen in Greece, but it happened across Europe and the world. In order to survive, they'd have to rely on other people to house them money, clothes and security as the state wouldn't help. However, luck would begin to change in 1760; in France a French priest called Charles Michel De L'Eppe created the world's first deaf school; the best part for the parents was that it was free. He developed a system that used finger spelling and signs. By 1788, he had published a French Sign Language dictionary.

In the seventeenth century, John Bulwer was an English Physician who wrote a series of books talking about deaf people; how they were living at the time and what could be done to make their lives easier in one of his books. He had the first pictures of signs that would've been used as sign language which has changed a lot since then. John Bulwer had the idea to build a school for deaf people; he understood the importance of giving deaf people an education which would give them independence and would help them achieve their goals and ambitions. John pushed for the plans to build a school for deaf people, but nothing was done about it until a century later.

In the eighteenth century, a man called Thomas Braidwood set up the first deaf school in Britain which was in Scotland, Edinburgh. It didn't help everyone though as it was only a school for the rich that could get their deaf children educated. But if they came from a poor family, they'd have to rely on family members or supportive people to educate them. At first, Thomas didn't know how to sign; he used oral methods to communicate and over time learnt sign language. He taught the children a combination of sign and oral methods. Children would do the signs and Thomas would take on board and use them for himself. He also didn't want to share his teaching methods much with other people. He believed that his teachings should remain in the family; so when his son becomes an adult, he would follow in his father's footsteps. Braidwood's school was really successful at the time. Many of his students were coming out of school succeeding in the wider world which was the first time in Britain. One of his students was Lord Seaforth; he was deaf but achieved great things in politics in becoming a MP in parliament.

From 1792 to the 1860s was the golden age of sign education and Braidwood's teaching methods would go on for another 100 years after he died. People started to realise that his method was a mixture of sign and oral methods also known as combined methods to teach deaf students. Heinicke from Germany believed that he could go one step further to teach deaf people to speak by using two of the human senses-touch and taste. For example, salt and vinegar were used to change the speech patterns. He believed that speech is what separates humans from animals, so by teaching them to speak, they would gain independence but also become more respected in society. However, Heinicke didn't always prove successful as it would've been harder for deaf people to understand as they would've needed the signs to understand what he would be teaching them.

Charles-Michel de l'Épée's teaching methods were also really successful; his students were well educated and literate. One of his students was called Pierre Desloges who later in life wrote a book about deaf education. He believed in the art of sign language so deeply that a new German method was made which would then go on to become one of the most popular sign language methods in the world. De L'Épée believed that sign language was the easiest to communicate new ideas. So much so that he found a way to encode the signs so that between him and his students, it would be easy to sign all in French. But Heinicke didn't believe in this method at all. He thought that as deaf people can make sounds from their mouths, they could speak. Both of them sent letters to each other arguing on the best method. Heinicke offered de L'Épée to teach his students his oral methods for six months which he declined because de L'Épée could teach pupils using sign language in just two weeks.

In the late nineteenth century, oralism started to gain popularity. The use of sign language was becoming ignored. Soma International Conference was set up in Milan in 1880 where there was a debate on which teaching methods were best. There was an argument that sign language damages the ability to speak, lip read and to think of ideas. Delegates went to a deaf school in 1880 and found that deaf pupils could speak very well; they decided that this is what they wanted-deaf people that could speak. There's no research to suggest that the pupils were born deaf or were just suffering with some hearing loss. One of the main reasons why people in society wanted deaf people to speak was because they'd be like normal people in society. The idea of a child to have any disability was scary to people which was why the popularity of oralism was high. The presentations were hugely in favour of oralism. As they believed if they could speak, they'd have the same opportunities as hearing children. There were fierce views on both sides of the argument. But there wasn't any research to suggest which method was the best as they both had their benefits. The debate was one sided as there wasn't a deaf person that attended the conference; 160 voted for oralism and just four against. This was the biggest betrayal in the deaf community because deaf people couldn't understand what they were learning through oralism, they would learn much quicker through sign. But after the Milan Conference, it was decided that sign language was no longer to be taught in schools, so years and years of no sign language would prove difficult for deaf students. What also happened after the Milan Conference, they wrote to all the major newspapers in the world on what happened in the dropping of the sign language method. However, many people started to believe that oralism was the best to teach deaf people. The teachers who had previously taught deaf people through sign language found themselves out of work as the new oral system was out into action.

Teachers weren't even taught sign language to teach their students anymore. Teachers were taught to use oralism. Some people who were in favour of sign language thought that it was an act of power and brainwashed people into thinking that this was the best way to teach. As students were only allowed to lip read for one hour, no sign language allowed which most deaf people hated as it was their main way to communicate. Deaf people were also made to think that speaking was bad, so it made them feel worthless in the class and even in the school playground. The classes only consisted of three lessons-speech, spelling and signing which would be alternated depending on the day. As the century moved on, oralism became more and more popular, so there was little room for signing at all. Teachers wouldn't sign at all; they would only speak and this would be so frustrating for deaf people as they wouldn't understand what they were saying.

Deaf people were expected to repeat what the teacher had said which wasn't 100% achievable as it was because they couldn't speak or fully understand the task, but when the teacher would be writing on the blackboard, the students would be secretly signing to each other behind their back so that people could understand if they were finding the lesson difficult.

Lip reading was hard for deaf students. Speech lessons would involve repeating what the teacher said through sound, for example, if the teacher said 'ahhhhh', the deaf child would repeat it while having the teacher's first two fingers to push the tongue to the roof of the mouth. If they thought that it would help them speak, then they were wrong. These lessons didn't make them use their brain because the teachers were doing it for them. Plus, I don't think having two fingers in your mouth teaches anyone anything. In this time period, there wasn't a full curriculum; it was just speech and spelling; they didn't learn any English maths or science. Like hearing students in the end, they felt like they weren't learning anything.

In the middle of the twentieth century, a new system came into action known as the Ewing System which had very strict views on oralism that teachers had to follow. If teachers didn't have the Ewing stand of approval for teaching them, they would be unemployed and therefore, it was for harder to find a teaching job. One of the examples of the Ewing method was to teach with no gestures, talking without body language. The Ewing System didn't give permission, or allowed teaching in any other way; it was their way or no way which made it harder for teachers without the ability to use sign language. Teachers were forced to teach deaf students how to speak which was almost torture for them because it was almost impossible to understand what the teacher was saying.

After WWII, new technology was introduced in helping deaf people even further which would revolutionise their world. The introduction of audiology was used to measure how good their hearing was which would come into categories profound, severe or partial hearing loss. Audiologists were there to help people with hearing loss. Hearing aids finally came into use to improve hearing which are still used today. Teachers also brought audiometry as a new lesson where pupils would put in headphones and they had to try and guess the word that they were hearing through the headphones; if a student got it wrong, the teacher would turn up the volume, so it was unbearable.

The sound would've been deafening without being born deaf. Despite sign language being banned in school, children would often sign in the playground in secret which made the rules of oralism more and more strict; if a student got caught signing on school grounds, they would be severely punished. One form of punishment was writing lines for one hour straight. Imagine writing 'I must not sign I must talk' for an hour nonstop. Another form of punishment was to be forced to wear a straight-jacket that would force your hand tucked under the waist and the teacher would tie it up behind the pupil's back, so that they couldn't sign any longer. Or they'd have their hands tied to their desk. No matter how hard the children tried to rebel against the Ewing System, they didn't have a voice that was strong enough; not even the teacher could rebel or ask to change it. Many deaf students who left school at this time were left mentally scared by their experiences, but sport activities and social network was excellent. Educationally, it was terrible letting many students down; it certainly wasn't a place to learn as a deaf child more like an area to be told what to do.

More deaf people had a better education by the time that they left school because they taught themselves or supportive family members. In the 1970s, a new report came into play discussing how the oral method of teaching simply failed deaf students because they left school without decent education and so, the opportunities outside of school were non-existent and something new needed to be done. In the start of the 1960s, there was an idea that deaf students could be taught in mainstream schools; this would give them more opportunities outside of school. At first, they only allowed partially deaf students into mainstream school, so that they could teach using oral methods; giving deaf students the chance to go to mainstream must've been a big leap for them because for the first time through society's eyes, they were seen as equals in the class rather people who were outcasts at the start of their history. That doesn't mean that it doesn't have its down points as being deaf isn't a learning disability, but they often learn slower. Having one less human sense can make learning harder and trickier to understand the teacher. Which would mean that they would need more support by a teaching assistant in the class or extra time to do their work in another class. But even today, extra support is limited; teaching assistants are often stretched to too many students who need extra help. Some are often left without help at all.

American Deaf Education History

Before deaf schools were built in the United States, the rich often heard how revolutionary the education system was in Europe for the deaf; so they sent their children to Europe to be educated. Whereas the poor would miss out. Many were sent to Thomas Braidwood's School and some went to France to learn as the school was free to the public at this time. There is one family in particular who endured the long trip to Europe-the Bolling family Thomas Bolling and his wife had three deaf children John, Mary and Thomas Jr.

John was the first child to be sent to Scotland to have Braidwood's expertise in 1771. A few months later, Mary and Thomas Jr came as well to the school. Thanks to Braidwood's teachings, they were exceedingly well in school. They travelled back to America in 1783 but sadly John, the eldest son suffered from an unknown illness and died on the 11 October 1783. Mary and Thomas Jr lived for another 40 years. The next generation wanted their children to be taught in America, so they needed to come with a plan to build a school. William who was Thomas and Elizabeth's youngest son married his first cousin and they had five children, two of whom were deaf. William's first son called William Albert helped drive William to create a school in America. So, he wrote to Thomas Braidwood's grandson John asking if he would travel to meet him in America to start building the new deaf school. John Braidwood arrived in America in 1812. John had plans of making the school similar to Thomas Braidwood's Academy for the deaf. After many setbacks, the school had finally been built in 1815, but it wasn't to last as Braidwood had personal struggles and Thomas Bolling couldn't financially keep it going, so the Cobbs School had to close in 1816.

The American School for the Deaf (ASD) is the oldest permanent school for the deaf in the United States; it was founded on 15 April 1817 in Hartford Connecticut by Thomas Gallaudet and Laurent Clerc. The school became supported by the state later in the year. It also became the first school in the country to win its first annual grant in 1819. But around 1815, Thomas Gallaudet had travelled across Europe as it was leading the way in teaching deaf people. Having visited Scotland and France, Thomas had gained methods and techniques of teaching which he brought back with him to the states. He went back and started plans to build the school. After the school was built, Thomas had convinced Laurent Clerc who was America's first deaf teacher to come and teach whereas Thomas could stay in the side lines of finances. While in Europe, Thomas wanted to learn Braidwood's teaching methods which the teaching committee at the time gladly did but he was sworn to secrecy that he wouldn't share any of the methods to anyone which he refused and left with the knowledge of his methods. He took what he learnt from Europe to America.

After a few months, Thomas ended up being the director of his new school. Classes started out small with only seven students in a class; throughout the remainder of the century, teachers like Laurent Clerc started teaching the deaf using sign language which is surprising because in the same century, the Milan Conference told every school that the oral method would be best to teach the deaf but it seemed that Gallaudet had his own ideas of keeping sign language going.

Around 40% of teachers were deaf and over 30 deaf schools were open by the end of the nineteenth century. In America, sign language was mainly used although teachers did try and teach deaf students the oral method. As schools grew, a change started to occur; a Civil War broke out in the 1850s. Sign language was popular amongst the deaf community. The hearing community thought that being deaf was isolating for them, as the people of America followed the Christian religion and beliefs, using sign language was the best way to communicate and be closer to God.

By the end of the Civil War, there was an argument based on Charles Darwin's theory of survival of the fittest. The one thing that kept humans and animals apart was talking. The idea was that talking gave deaf people more opportunities and power to be more successful in society. If they signed all their life, they wouldn't be able to gain independence; also it was not humanlike. More schools stared opening up for the deaf in the late 1860s but this time, there would be oral methods only. Deaf students weren't allowed to sign at all because the hearing community began to think that signing would be a threat to them, so they preferred the oral method which was to the offence of deaf people; they didn't like it one bit because signing was the easiest way for them to communicate. Oralists believed that signing made deaf people abnormal but by teaching a deaf person to talk would make them normal despite their disabilities. If they thought that it would stop them from signing, they would have to think again. In fact, it inspired them to sign more because it was the easiest way to communicate a way that they could understand each other. But this would prove to be difficult for the hearing community as they didn't like it and didn't want to integrate with deaf people whilst they would sign.

In 1880, there was a Congress on the education of the deaf. It was an international meeting of deaf educators from seven countries. There were five delegates from America and 164 in total. It was organised by the Pereire Society, a group that was against sign language. More than half who were invited were oralists. Therefore, the Congress was again pretty one-sided like the Milan Congress which came as no surprise that oral methods were voted in favour instead of sign language and an agreement was set to all seven countries (Italy,

France, UK, America, Sweden, Belgium and Germany) that the oral method ought to be preferred than signs for educating instructions to the deaf. It was a devastating blow for deaf people in this time period as they preferred signing.

In the 1890s, deaf education in the United States was only limited to children but with the help of Lillie Eginton Warren and her assistant Edward B Nichie education was expanded to deaf adults. In the early part of the twentieth century, after the Congress, the new rule of only allowing the oral method was put into place and whoever tried to sign in class or outside of school would be punished. Teachers who taught sign language would've lost their jobs; teachers who solely taught oral methods would be swapped in their position. Even deaf teachers weren't allowed to teach anymore; only teachers that could hear were allowed. Throughout the century, schools that were teaching sign language were becoming less and less existent whereas oral schools were becoming more and more popular. The main goal that teachers had for deaf students was to prepare them for the real world. The hearing world which required them to learn English and learn how to lip read. All deaf students were strictly taught the oral method and restricted sign language. But they still continued to sign anyway as long as they wouldn't get caught. One form of punishment if they got caught was to put on white gloves but they were tied onto the hands so they couldn't get them off which restricted movement in the fingers and hands. Or if a student wasn't doing very well in class, they'd be sent to a manual school, but they would have in their school report a failure. This was considered a dark time to be a deaf student.

Towards the late twentieth century, the oral method was still as popular as when it first started but then in the 1960s, Roy Kay Holcomb came up with a different way which he called total communication where instead of forcing to teach deaf students oralism, he came up with the idea to let the student pick their own way to learn. Because he found that if you allow the student to make their own choices on their learning, then you'll get a better outcome in the long run. This meant that a student could use their preferred method of learning, which was great because if one teaching method didn't work then they would keep changing it for the individual until they could learn better.

In 1988, the president of the Gallaudet University had stepped down from his role and voting for a new president had started for only three candidates, two who of who were deaf and one could hear. The results came through, not publicly but secretly when they eventually found out that their new president was a hearing one. The deaf community went out on a march and took matters into their own hands. There had been marches in the deaf community before but not a protest such as this one. Students made signs and gave demonstrations like the common protest you'd see today. Some students had locked the school gates late at night. Some refused to even go to school. Just a few weeks later, the president stepped down and a new one was re-elected. King Jordan was the first deaf president of Gallaudet University. The deaf education system vastly improved. Deaf people were pursuing and earning their advanced degrees. Also, in schools throughout America, students demanded deaf teachers, superintendents and administrators and new teaching programs were created for the deaf not only in America but across the world such as Japan, South Africa, Sweden etc. Having a deaf president in Gallaudet University not only changed the education system in America but also the entire world. In many ways, America really modernised and helped the lives of deaf people worldwide.

In 1990, the invention of the cochlear implant was introduced to children aged between one and two which revolutionised not only their education but their life as well. The implant was surgically placed inside the ear canal which provides a sense of sound working with the cochlea and the hearing nerve. The sound travelled the very small wires which were connected to the implant allowing the patient to hear. In education, more and more children with the implant weren't being taught in schools that taught sign language, but they were taught in mainstream schools back to the oral program without extra support. Parents were not encouraged to sign because it was feared that it may slow down their speech which in fact wasn't true at all. As mainstream schools were on the rise; this caused the downfall for signing as many deaf students could attend mainstream schools. Today, many students are taught through an Individualised Education Program (IEP); individual needs of students are different, so having their own program meets their needs, along with meeting the requirements of what the state asks from the teachers.

Important People Throughout Deaf History

John Bulwer was born in London; he remained in this great city all his life. It is uncertain where he was educated but some suspect that he went to Oxford University. He was a son of a chemist Thomas Bulwer and his mother Marie Evans. After her death in 1638, John inherited some property in St Albans to which gave him a small income. During the Civil War, John stopped working as a physician and concentrated on his study and writing. He wrote a collection of

John Bulwer 16 May 1606–1 October 1656 Author of Deaf History (Father of sign Language)

five books from 1640 to 1653. These books talked about the first of their kind; no one had thought about deaf people in the way that John did. In his book called *Chirologia and Chironomia* with Chirologia meaning (natural language of the hand) and using gestures of common Chironomia meaning (natural hand gestures) was based on his idea that hands could have a language by their own. Using different gestures with the hands could mean that anyone could understand, including the deaf which was the start of sign language as we know today. In his words, 'the hand speaks all languages, and as universal character of reason is generally understood and known by all nations, among the formal differences of their tongue. And being the only speech that is natural to man, it may well be called the tongue and general language of human nature, which, without teaching, men in all regions of the habitable world though at the first sight most easily understand'.

His book called *Philocophus* was about his idea on teaching the deaf by setting up the first academy for the deaf but let's just say it didn't go very well. Other men around him and even his closest friends thought that he was mad as deaf people were considered dumb in this time. But that didn't stop him from having his theories; just before he wrote the book, he started to walk around London meeting other deaf people and how they were living at the time. He had the idea that the muscles surrounding the eye could also be a way to communicate accompanied with the mouth, and that the body had a whole range of senses. John was onto the idea that communication doesn't always have to be from eyes and ears but there were so many other ways for people to communicate. John went on to write another three books on humans' anatomy. Later on, in life, he adopted a little girl named Chirothea Johnson.

Thomas Braidwood was born in Scotland and he was the fourth child to parents called Thomas and Agnes Braidwood where his parents owned a farm which was called Hill Head Farm in Covington in south Lanarkshire. He learnt his skills to become a teacher at Edinburgh University then he managed to get a teaching job. Thomas's main subject was writing but he was pretty good at most subjects as well. In 1760, Alexander Sheriff had a deaf son called Charles and he wanted a good teacher that would help him get a good education. Alexander knew Thomas as he was a maths teacher himself. He wanted his son to learn to write. Thomas had accepted but his services didn't come cheap though; he only taught the wealthy families of this time. After a few years, Thomas had successfully taught Charles how to write. In doing so, he got an idea to change his career where he wanted to just teach the deaf. He renamed his school Braidwood's Academy for the Deaf and Dumb. This was the first school of its kind in Britain, Thomas used a variety of methods to teach the deaf; he knew by using a combination of sign language and lip reading, he would be getting the best results from his students. Soon after, Thomas moved to Hackney in the eastern outskirts of London, and it was here that he expanded his potential as a deaf teacher. He opened up a new academy using the same name in Grove House off Mare Street. Thomas's cousin Joseph Watson became the first headteacher at the asylum for the deaf on Old Kent Road in Bermondsey. Thomas married Margaret Pearson on 1 October 1752, and they had three daughters, all born in Edinburgh-Margaret, Elizabeth and Isabella. All three daughters shared the same passion as Thomas had in teaching. Isabella took up the academy when Thomas sadly died in Hackney 1806.

Thomas Braidwood
(1715–24 October 1806)
(Founder of the first school for the Deaf in the UK)

Charles De L'Epee
24 November 171–23
December 1789
Founder of the first
School for the deaf

Charles De L'Epee was born in Yvelines, Versailles France on 24 November 1712. Charles grew up into a wealthy family. He studied to be a catholic priest and then after studying, he did some charitable work for the poor. One day, he was out in Paris and he saw the terrible conditions that were prevalent at the time. He met two deaf sisters who were communicating to him using sign language. From that moment on, he decided to dedicate his life to education and salvation of deaf people. In 1760, he founded his school for the deaf which happens to be the oldest school in the world. He believed that deaf people were capable of language and by giving deaf people the power of education and wellbeing, they would avoid going to hell as they believed in those days. Charles's school was not only the oldest, but it was the first school in the world to be free for the deaf. Charles started to set up a system were French language could be translated into French sign language. Eppe's original interest was religious education. By influencing people through religion, he was able to convince the deaf to use sign language more in society which worked in his favour as for the first time, deaf people could communicate with strangers and even stand up for themselves in a court. A few years later, France would be in a new era in its history; the French Revolution in 1789 but sadly Charles died in the beginning of the revolution.

Legacy

Charles's body was put into a tomb and put into the Church of Saint Roch in Paris which you can still see today. Two years after his death, the National Assembly recognised him a 'benefactor to humanity' which was an honour for the work that he did for the deaf. That wasn't all; the assembly also learnt that deaf people also had rights as hearing people did from the declaration of the rights of man. In 1791, the Institution National des Sourds-Muets à Paris which L'Eppe helped establish and also fought for funding from the government for funding became known as the Institut National de Jeunes Sourds de Paris (National Institute of Young Deaf Paris) which would go on to help the deaf and more importantly, generations to come.

Samuel Heinicke was born in <u>Nautschutz</u>, Germany in 1927. Samuel went to a village school when he was young and he enrolled himself in the army. In his free time, he had a passion for books and reading. He mainly read books based on language as he loved learning different languages. He could fluently speak German, French and Latin. He also began to teach these languages to other people. He came across one book that changed his life which was called *The Talking Deaf* by a Swiss physician called Johann Konrad Amman which really captured his imagination. So much so that he went from teaching language to other people to teaching the deaf. The book was about teaching deaf people the ability to lip read, learning the ability to talk; by watching other people and moving their own lips over time, they'd be able to speak.

Samuel Heinicke
10 April 1727–30 April 1790
Founder of the Oral method of Teaching

In 1756, a seven-year war broke out in Germany and was taken prisoner by the Prussians; this was a setback in Samuel's teaching but luckily, he managed to escape in the middle of the war and became secretary to the Danish ambassador which was in his favour as in 1769, the ambassador helped Samuel secure a teaching position near Eppendorf, where he found his calling to become a deaf teacher. In 1778, Heinicke opens his first German school for the deaf. He insisted that lip reading was the best way, because his students could speak and understand the language as it was in society. He bitterly opposed sign language so much that he published a book attacking Charles de L'Eppe. In addition to his work, he was an advocate for the oral method and promoted his methods throughout Europe. He also promoted the Phonetic method of teaching which involves teaching children the alphabet with their own sounds which are combined phonetically allowing children to learn words so that they can combine words to read and this is still used today. Twelve years after Heinicke set up his school for the deaf, he sadly died in 1790. His wife continued running the school in his memory, he had his face on a German postage stamp in 1778 in honour of his work for the deaf in East Germany.

William Willard was born on 1 November in Brattleboro in Vermont; then his parents decided to move up north to Rockingham in Vermont where most of

William Willard
1 November 1809–15 February 1881
The First Deaf Principal in America

his childhood was spent. William was born deaf and his parents managed to get him into the American School for the Deaf in Connecticut where he was taught by Laurent Clerc (father of deaf education). After he graduated, he decided to follow in Laurent's footsteps in becoming a teacher. He went to the Ohio School for the Deaf, where not only did he get his first job, but he also met his future wife, Eliza Young who was also deaf and a teacher. A few years later, William proposed to Eliza and then soon after they married and set off to Indianapolis. This is where they had the idea to set up their own school for the deaf and they set out recruiting students in order to set it up. To which they succeeded and in the first day which was the 1st of October 1843. William's school had twelve students; eventually Indiana passed a law which allowed William and Eliza to start the school and be recognised throughout the state. William became principal of his school. Soon after, the state passed another law which officially declared Indiana School for the Deaf as the sixth state school for the deaf. More importantly, it would be provided for free for families in need for their children's education. William died on 15 February 1881 leaving an important part of deaf history; it was certainly vital that he taught so many for deaf students to have a voice. Throughout Williams and Eliza's long and happy marriage, they had six children;

Legacy

William's legacy is one of the more important parts of deaf history; without him, the growth rate of deaf schools would've happened a lot slower; thanks to his work, deaf people have the power of education in America.

*Thomas Hopkins
Gallaudet
10 December 1787–10
September 1851
Founder of Deaf
Education in America*

Thomas Hopkins Gallaudet was born on 10 December 1787 in Philadelphia, Pennsylvania. He was really well educated, and he went to Yale university with very high qualifications. In 1808, he got his master's degree. He also had interests studying law trade and theology. He had offers in working in these fields, but he declined due to his concerns for his health. However, it was soon after that he developed an interest in education; to be more specific educating the deaf. Thomas would often hear in newspapers about how the European methods of teaching the deaf were so well known throughout the world, so he travelled to Europe to see what kind of methods they were. His first stop was in Scotland only because he had heard of a deaf teacher called Thomas Braidwood who was famous all over the world for his teaching methods but sadly Thomas had already died before Gallaudet had the chance to meet him, so he met his son John Braidwood and he taught and shared his father's teaching methods with him. But there was a family tradition that the methods would be kept secret to which Gallaudet agreed. After getting an idea of Braidwood's teaching methods, he set of to France where he got taught De L'Eppe's sign language and communication from Roch-Ambroise Cucurron Sicard (Royal Head of the institute of the deaf) where he was invited. In 1816, Thomas arrived back in America after his European trip. Thomas used his inspiration to build his own school in America for the deaf. With the help of Laurent Clerc, they both managed to raise the money to establish the asylum for the deaf and mutes in Hartford, Connecticut. This would later become known as American School for the Deaf. The US Congress granted them land grant in support of Thomas and Laurent's work. For more than 50 years, this school has been the main facility which was used to teach deaf students. In 1821, Thomas married one of his former students Sophia Fowler and they had eight children together. In 1830, Gallaudet retired from teaching but later on was invited to professorship in New York University. In 1833, Thomas proposed special training for future deaf teachers that would like to teach. Thomas also wrote textbooks of his experiences in teaching deaf students.

Laurent Clerc
26 December 1785–18
July 1869
First Deaf Teacher in
American Education

Laurent Clerc was born east of Lyon in a small village called La Balme in France on 26 December 1785; his parents were called Joseph-François Clerc and Marie-Élisabeth Candy. His father was the mayor of La Balme. He was born into a very normal family but one day when he was just one years of age, something would change his life forever. Laurent was just playing around like any other child until he fell of a chair into the fireplace causing severe burns to his head and face. Laurent's family believed that this accident caused him to lose not only his hearing but his sense of smell as well. After the severe burns got better, he still had a scar on his right cheek which he would have for the rest of his life. However, despite what his family, Laurent believed that he was born deaf and had lost the sense of smell, which is reason why the accident happened. Clerc attended the National Institute for the Young Deaf People in Paris as a student and later became a teacher there too. As a student, he was taught by Abbe Sicard and Jean Massieu.

In 1815, Laurent, Abbe and Jean travelled to England where they gave a lecture on deaf education. By coincidence, Thomas Gallaudet was there as he was searching for other deaf teachers who would be willing to help him set up his deaf school in America. In 1816, Thomas Gallaudet was invited to the National Institute for the Young Deaf People. This really inspired Thomas, especially the way the students were being taught and the way that children were interacting with each other in the class. After only a few months, Thomas invited Laurent to come to America to help him set up his school for the deaf. Laurent was naturally hesitant at first because he didn't want to leave his home and his life he already had in France. But Thomas kept persuading him to come; eventually, Laurent accepted and they crossed the sea to America. During the journey to America, Laurent was taught English by Thomas as he knew very little and Laurent taught Thomas sign language. So, they both helped each other establishing The American School for the Deaf on 15 April 1817. Laurent was the main teacher at the school and was highly praised for his work whereas Thomas Gallaudet took over the finances and maintenance of the school. Laurent passed away on 18 July 1869; he was 83 he served more than 50 years in

Hartford, Connecticut. His work made him respected and loved by the community

Legacy

Laurent Clerc became one the leading figures throughout deaf education in America despite not being able to speak or hear. He was a pioneer in teaching sign language and getting students to have a high level of education for his time.

Roy Kay Holcomb
24 July 1923–26
November 1998
Founder of the Total
Communication
Method

Roy Kay Holcomb was born on 24 July 1923 to a poor family with seven other siblings. Roy was also born deaf, but no one really knew that until he was 9 years old. Roy went to the Texas school for the deaf, then later on, he went to Gallaudet College as it was known at the time where he got his bachelor's degree in 1947. He then went to the University of Tennessee where he got his special master's degree. Later, he got a third master's degree in sociology from Ball State University. The Texas school of the deaf had a very strict military regime. Roy found it particularly hard to keep up while he was a student there. The school was founded in 1856 and throughout its history, it went through a few name changes from Texas Institution for the Deaf and Dumb to Texas Deaf and Dumb Institution to Texas Deaf and Dumb Asylum. Finally, they kept with the name the Texas School for the Deaf which still remains today. The school was so poor that throughout a civil war, it could hardly pay the teachers' salaries properly. Years later, the school eventually got more financial help from the government and was able to be run properly. Roy had an interest in sports; he played baseball and basketball. His one true hobby was basketball so much so that he pursued it further at Gallaudet University; he was part of the team called the Blue Bison's nicknamed the five iron men as they played in all three matches in the tournament. They played in the Mason Dixon Conference tournament which they won; Roy was the leading scorer in the Blue Bison where he got his nickname the iron man. Roy later became an administrator which is where he promoted total communication. He also became a teacher and coach at South Dakota School for the Deaf 1947–1955. Then he went on to teaching in Tennessee School for the Deaf 1955–1961 where he also helped supervise the deaf education program. Then he moved again to Santa Ana in California 1968 to 1973 where he was a director for various deaf community services until 1985. After graduating from Gallaudet University in 1947, he got married to Marjorie Bell Stakley; both of them had similar interests in studying, writing, and teaching. Together they had two deaf sons who they both loved dearly. On thanksgiving, 1998 Roy died of Parkinson's disease at the age of 75.

Legacy

Roy really helped modernise deaf education through his revolutionary total communication methods where oralism had been dominating deaf education for a century. Roy opened up not just one way for deaf children to learn but multiple ways by signing, writing, oralism etc. which gave deaf students freedom in the classroom and that is something to be proud of.

Alice Cogswell
31 August 1805–30 December 1830
One of the first Deaf Students in American Deaf Education History.
Thomas Gallaudet's Inspiration for the creation of the American School for the deaf

Alice Cogswell is quite special considering she only lived for 25 years; she had a massive impact on the beginning of deaf education. She was born on 31 October 1805 in Hartford, Connecticut. At the age of two, she had spotted fever which is called measles or meningitis today. which lead to her getting Cerebral meningitis. The illness took her hearing and her ability to speak. At this time in history, deafness was considered as a mental health issue and people thought that you were dumb and couldn't be taught. Her father Dr Cogswell was really sad that he couldn't talk to his daughter as for the first part of her life, she was really silent. She would spend some of her time looking out the window watching other children playing with her brothers and sisters. Her siblings didn't speak to her as they believed that deaf children couldn't talk.

Thomas Gallaudet moved in only next door to Alice when she was 9 years old. Thomas was also friends with her parents; he couldn't help but notice that Alice wasn't interacting with the other children in the playground she would just sit and watch on her own. He asked her parents why, to which he was informed that she was deaf. Thomas was intrigued by this, so he decided to spend some time with her to cheer her up. They both spent a lot of time drawing pictures together which really showed Thomas how talented and smart Alice was. Soon after, Thomas decided to teach Alice by coming over to her house in the afternoons. He would teach her how to read and write which Alice learnt particularly fast knocking down all the stereotypes that previously shadowed deaf people. Alice's progress was a slow ongoing process as Thomas's methods didn't always work as he didn't know how to teach a deaf child, as his methods went by trial and error. A few years later, Thomas and her father Dr Mason Cogswell both shared the idea of building a school for the deaf as they thought it would be best for Alice's progress in education.

Thomas and Mason found that there were over 40 children living in Connecticut that were deaf and more in other states. With this newfound information, Thomas had the idea to go to Europe where there was loads of schools for the deaf at this time and where he could learn the methods of teaching deaf children and build a deaf school back in America. Thomas Gallaudet set out to sea to go to Europe where deaf schools already existed. During his time in Europe, Alice attended a hearing school which was ok but it wasn't brilliant for her education as she couldn't understand the teachers because she couldn't hear them and there were no methods for teaching the deaf students at this time. Alice was a very lively person; she enjoyed many things reading and writing, sewing and dancing; she would love it when her parents would put on a party. Alice was particularly good at mimicking others and loved music. After spending some time in Europe, Thomas Gallaudet came back to America and he brought with him a new friend Laurent Clerc. They set out creating the American School for the Deaf. Alice was the first student along with six other. In 1830, Alice's father died; Alice was deeply upset with the news and just 13 days later, Alice died at the age of 25; some people at the time thought she died of a broken heart.

Legacy

Alice was the person that shined the light for deaf people in America and she gave inspiration to Thomas Gallaudet to build a school for deaf society to be proud of in the long run. Without Alice's legacy, the American school for the Deaf may have been built but it may have been forgotten for anther few decades; so, she really improved the lives of deaf people not just educationally but as people as well. Alice broke down so many stereotypes and allowed hearing people to see how smart a deaf person can be.

History of Hearing Aids

Throughout the years, deaf people have always needed assistance with understanding communication. The first way often gets overlooked; sometimes people used to use our eyes to read the mouth movements. This wasn't always 100% accurate but it gave deaf people a vague understanding of speech which is what all they had at the time. It wasn't until the seventeenth century that new inventions came into play.

Throughout years, there have been many advances of hearing technology that have made a massive impact on deaf people's lives; although in the earlier years many deaf people didn't use them because they looked stupid or they just didn't work at all. In the later part of the seventeenth century, hearing trumpets were the first invention to help with hearing. They were the hearing aids of their time and by strengthening the sound waves that travelled through the outer part of the trumpet into the inner ear canal, these allowed people to hear as the sound waves vibrated in the ear drums. The earlier trumpets were made out of sheet metal, and silver and were the expensive options at the time, or they were made out of wood and animal horns for poorer families. As time progressed, technology advanced and created new electric hearing aids that became available in the twentieth century. An American called Miller Reese Hutchison developed the first digital hearing aid which was based on the idea of the first telephones. Miller called it the Akouphone; the inspiration was a childhood friend who lost his hearing due to Scarlett fever (bacterial disease). Miller studied electrical engineering and went to medical college in Alabama University to study the anatomy of the ear which would play a vital role in making a hearing aid. The Akouphone used carbon transmitters and electrical currents to amplify audio signals. The only downside was that it wasn't portable and quite heavy to move around. The people using it were left tethered to it and were unable to move away from a bulky machine.

At the start of the twentieth century, vacuum tubes were invented which was a technological breakthrough of its time for hearing aids. The vacuum tube worked by transferring electric currents from batteries to the hearing aids to power them. The tubes were a massive success throughout the beginning of the twentieth century until transistors took over in the late 1940s. It could do two things-it could be an amplifier where it would take a weak electric current also known as an input and then makes the current stronger when the current came out if the output. This was very useful for hearing aids as they helped power the tiny microphone which helped pick up sound from the world around them and then the transistor powered a loudspeaker so that deaf people could hear better.

Now , coming to modern digital heading aids. In the late twentieth century, computer science changed everything as computer simulation was widely used mainly for audio processing. The computer had software called (BLODI) which stands for block of compiled diagrams. The software couldn't process audio in real time, but it could process any sound system in a block diagram format which helped build a special phone for people with hearing impairments. In 1967, Harry Levitt used BLODI to simulate a hearing aid on a computer. Then years later, a new hearing aid was made called the Quasi digital hearing aid which allowed both analogue and digital components to be combined into a single compact case. It also had a digital controller which controlled the analogue components (amplifiers, filters and signal limiters); the hearing aid was successful from a practical point of view in the sense that it didn't need much power to function and was compact at the same time. At this time, analogue amplifier technology was created which worked well with the semiconductor chips which were also built for digital cameras. DHA heading aids started to become more popular; they were small enough to fit into the ear. For the first time, the hearing aid could actually fit inside the ear rather than wearing earphones attached to an electronic box. Also, the new digital hearing aids had a microprocessor which processed the sound around which completely replaced the analogue components (amplifier limiters and filters). This also allowed hearing aids to be programmable which meant that it could adjust by itself and also allowed advanced programming such as sound reduction. Further developments on digital hearing aids in the 1980s were about making them smaller and compact and allowing the microprocessors to process sound in real time. Small microchips have been created since 1987 allowing the hearing aid to be compact and discreet on the ear which is similar to how they are today.

Is Deafness Genetic?

Around a century back, there would've been a debate on deafness was caused by a gene mutation or whether it was just through the environment around. Well, at first, we only believed that it was only an environmental cause. Even if no one in your family before you was not deaf, it didn't mean that it won't affect future generations as our genes have their own rules. Science has discovered that there is two types of deafness resulting through genes. The first one being non-syndromic and the second syndromic deafness.

Non-Syndromic simply means that it causes deafness before birth with no physical changes in our genes, but syndromic deafness means that you are born deaf with a gene mutation and other changes in the body. The genes to look out for are DFNA, DFNB and DFNX. DFNA is a gene mutation. One gene in particular that stands out for deafness is GJB2. GJB2 is a gene which tells the cells in the inner ear to make a protein which is important in processing sounds to hear. However, this gene can be mutated and can cause hearing loss before birth. Bear in mind that it is not just the GJB2 gene that causes deafness; there are more than 100 types of GJB2 genes which can mutate and cause the same thing, but there are two main types-one is DFNB1 and DFNA3; both are the gene mutations of the gene GJB2 and they are also inherited from parents. Regarding the DFNB1 mutation, this is where two copies of the GJB2 gene are mutated inside its cell in chromosome 13. This causes non-syndromic hearing loss which ranges from mild to severe hearing loss. There are around 50% of cases to which the GJB2 gene copies itself. Other mutations happen when the DFNB1 mutation deletes or inserts DNA building blocks within the GJB2 gene which is the most common cause.

Particularly in the north of Europe, DFNB1 deletes on base pair at position 35 in the GJB2 gene. In Asian countries, the same thing happens but in a different place in our chromosomes (position 235). Now from Jewish ancestry, this is where it gets interesting, because the DFNB1 mutation deletes only a single base in a different area if the chromosome (position 167) which is common in the Jewish countries. This is rare though, but it can happen when the gene GJB2 mutation that causes the DFNB1 to replace a base pair with an incorrect gene or deletes a gene from the DNA. As a whole, the gene mutations that are caused by DFNB1 are often described as loss of function. So, it means that the inner ear doesn't have the function to process sound; therefore you'll end up having hearing loss. Now DFNA3 is again inherited but this time, it's only a copy of one mutated version of the GJB2 gene. This form of hearing loss can happen either before birth (pre-lingual) or after the child learns how to speak (post-lingual). The hearing range depends in the individual, but it can be between mild or severe. It may affect the person to hear high frequency sounds. Over time, this condition can get worse for the individual, the GJB2 gene mutations that causes DFNA3 replaces the correct amount of protein with the wrong amount of protein in the inner ear which is described as 'dominant negative', which means the individual has an abnormal version of the GJB2 gene which prevents the formation of any functional gap junctions. This may affect the survival of cells in the inner ear. Now, I'd like to finish off this chapter by celebrating a few deaf people who have strived to do great things in their life.

Famous Deaf People

*Ludwig Van Beethoven
16 December 1770–
26 March 1827
One of the greatest composers of all time*

Let's start with one of the greatest ever known composers of all time **Ludwig Van Beethoven**. Ludwig was born in Bonn in Western Germany. Ludwig showed from an early age his musical talent that his dad vigorously taught him. His father Johann Van Beethoven was extremely strict by the time Ludwig was four years old. Johann made Ludwig play the piano so that the family could get out of poverty. Over time, Johann became more of a dictator towards Ludwig rather than a father, so much so that Johann placed all of the family's wellbeing on his young shoulders. Johann would also use anything to get Ludwig to listen to his father such as beating him, locking him in small spaces, which Ludwig hated him but also feared him more. Ludwig's mother was more loving towards him but throughout her life, she suffered chronic depression and fatigue. She would try her best to protect him from his violent father but wouldn't always succeed as he was so dominating. The relationship between Ludwig's parents wasn't loving towards each other. It would be really rare that you'd see them show their love. One of the reasons why Ludwig's mother was depressed because she had a very challenging life. When Ludwig mother was 16 years, she had married a man and they had a son but sadly the baby died at infancy; then only two years later, her husband died. After these events, she met and married Johann Van Beethoven. At the start of their marriage, the family lost four children in infancy before Ludwig was born and two younger brothers survived Kaspar Anton Karl van Beethoven (baptised 8 April 1774–15 November 1815) and Nikolaus Johann, the youngest, was born on 2 October 1776. Ludwig's first teacher was his father, and this was when he would use threatening behaviour to get him to play the piano; it wouldn't matter what time of the day. He later went on to have other music teachers. An organist Gilles Van Eeden, Tobias Friedrich Pfeiffer, a family friend who provided keyboard tuitions, and Franz Rovantini who instructed Ludwig to play the violin. Outside of the teaching when Ludwig was only five years old, Tobias Pfeiffer also had a strict regime like his father making him stay up late to practice. Sometimes, he would be dragged out of bed just to play the keyboard; this regime made the young Beethoven come close to tears due the harsh treatment that he got. Ludwig's father was also aware of another great composer Wolfgang Mozart; he was also friends with his father Leopold Mozart. Leopold and Johann worked hard to promote the young Beethoven as a child prodigy outing up posters in the local area and when he was just seven years old; he had performed for the first time in March 1778.

Beethoven Hearing Loss

No one truly knows the cause but there have certainly been rumours over the years; some people think that he suffered from an epileptic seizure when he woke up from his seizure, he suffered really bad tinnitus which began to get worse over time. Other theories are he suffered with lead poisoning. His autopsy results also had theories of their own as well rumour had it that he had distended the inner ear which developed small lesions over time. Also, another rumour straight after he died, his autopsy found that he contracted typhus (spotted fever) in the summer of 1796. What was also intriguing in his autopsy report was that there was a really high level of lead in his system; no one knows what the cause of that was and why people used lead. But what we do know is that the lead would've made Beethoven's mood swings more erratic. Another theory for his hearing loss was that a mixture of Beethoven's bad health when he was older and lead poisoning was the cause of his hearing loss.

Later Years

Beethoven still continued to write and make music despite hearing loss; he wrote and composed all of his nine symphonies without his complete hearing; that's if the theory of typhus is true. While he was deaf, his quality of social life was challenging as he couldn't hear people speak and he couldn't read lips either. He would write letters to his closest friends to say how miserable being deaf was

Hellen Adams Keller
27 June 1880–1 June
1968
Author, Political
Activist, Lecturer

making him as hearing was the only and best human sense for music. Suicide did cross his mind, so he took to drinking a lot and also as a way of medicating his depression but it didn't work. Beethoven died on 27 March 1827. There are theories on how he died but the most popular one was when his autopsy was done it was discovered the Beethoven died of post-hepatitic cirrhosis of the liver at the age of 56. He may have had a short life in terms of today's standards but the ever-lasting legacy to create music which helped him to keep living and help inspire to change people's lives.

Hellen Keller was born in Tuscumbia in Alabama she was the oldest of two daughters of Arthur H Keller and Katherine Keller. Hellen also had two stepbrothers. Her father served as an officer in the confederate army during the civil war. Her family wasn't that wealthy as their main income was from their cotton plantation. Later, Arthur became the editor of a local newspaper in north Alabamian. When Hellen was born, she was a healthy baby girl; she had all her senses-she could see, hear, talk but when she was just two years old, she was struck by an illness which would change her life forever. This illness known at the time as brain fever where a part of the brain became inflamed. As a result, she would live the rest of her life being both deaf and blind. When she was around seven years old, she met one of her closest friends Martha Washington. Martha was the daughter of the family cook; the two had created a new type of sign language. This would involve signing in one hand whilst touching one of Helen's hands, so she could feel the movements and the shapes of the letters that were being said. In Hellen's earlier years, she would be considered as a wild child kicking and screaming. At one point, the screaming got so bad that people thought about putting her into an institution. She was only expressing her frustration at learning how to communicate without sight or hearing as progress was slow. Things were about to change as her mother was seeking inspiration, she noticed a travelogue by Charles Dickens in which was an article about the successful teachings of Laura Bridgman. Hellen's mother and her father headed to Baltimore, Maryland to see a specialist. They saw Dr J Julian Chisolm; after examining Hellen, he suggested that she went and see

146

Alexander Graham Bell who invented the telephone but he was also working with deaf people at the time and he suggested that Hellen should go to the institution for the blind in Massachusetts. The family met the school's director Michael Anagnos. He suggested that Hellen should work with the school's most recent graduates. Anne Sullivan who came to her aid, helped her make sense of the world by teaching her how to communicate; this would be the start of their 49 years relationship.

On 3 March 1887, Anne went to Hellen's home in Alabama. Anne taught her finger spelling to get her to understand the word doll because she had bought one for her but tensions grew as Hellen began to get frustrated because she wasn't able to understand it. As Hellen's frustration grew, Anne thought it would be best if Hellen would be isolated from her family so that she could solely concentrate on her teachings. So, Anne found a cottage where she moved in with Hellen; the very first word that Hellen learnt was water and Anne encouraged her and guided her towards the local water pump; she placed Hellen's right hand under the water and as the water was running over her hand, Anne spelt the word w-a-t-e-r on her left hand to which she understood as she repeated it on Anne's hand. Anne and Hellen worked tirelessly all day and moved onto other objects that Anne would place in her hand; by nightfall Hellen had learnt 30 words through sign language. Things immediately started to change for Hellen. From then on, she managed to attend speech classes at Boston School for the Deaf.

I can't help but think it must've been daunting at first; not being able to see or hear the teacher but Anne was there by her side so that she was able to translate what the teacher was saying. She spent 25 years to try to perfect the skill of speech so that others could understand her. Then from 1894 to 1896, she attended the New York School for the Deaf and it was here she started learning regular subjects that you and I would learn in class. In 1896, Hellen was determined to further her education; it had been her dream to attend college, so she did just that she attended Cambridge School for Young Ladies. She also became an icon in her own right as her life story leaked out into the community. With this, she met some famous people at the time; one of them was a writer called Mark Twain he was so impressed by her story that they became friends and he introduced her to one of his friends Henry H Rodgers who was a rich man and made his money in the oil business. Henry was impressed with Hellen's story and her talents and drive. Mark offered to pay for Hellen's education fees at Cambridge School.

Activism

After finishing college, she wanted to know more about the world around her and how she could make the world a better place; more news spread about her life story from Massachusetts to New England. She would become a local celebrity. By this time, she was a keen lecturer, talking about her life experiences being both deaf and blind but also the downfalls that society makes life challenging for disabled people. Throughout the first half of the twentieth century, she wanted to tackle both social and political issues, including women's rights, promoting peace for all and birth control. She testified against the congress and worked to improving the lives of those who were blind. By 1920, she had helped co-found George Kessler International to combat the causes and consequences of blindness and malnutrition.

In 1920, she helped found the American Civil Liberties Union which protected the rights for all human beings in America and it does still to this day. When the American Federation for the Blind was established in 1921, Hellen had effective national outlets for her efforts, she became a member in 1924 and participated in many campaigns to raise awareness, money and support for the blind. She also joined other organisations that were there to help the less fortunate, including the permanent blind war relief fund which is called the American Braille Press today). Soon after she finished college, she also joined the socialist party which was following one of Hellen's friends John Macy. Whilst being a part of the party, she wrote a lot of articles about socialism between 1909 and 1921. She very much supported the party's president Eugene Debs, one of Helen's articles was called out of the dark which gave the public a sense of what she stood for on socialism and works affairs. In 1936, Hellen's beloved teacher and companion Anne Sullivan died; she had been suffering from health problems for several years and by 1932 she lost her eyesight completely. But all was not lost for Hellen as a young woman called Polly Thomson who was first Hellen's and Anne's secretary in 1914 and decided to be there for Hellen like Anne did; she became her constant companion.

In 1946, she was appointed counsellor for the American Foundation for the Blind overseas. Between 1946–1957, she had travelled to 35 countries and five continents gaining more fans around the world; one country in particular however had a special place in its heart for Hellen. This was Japan; before Helen arrived in Japan, it had been bombed by the Americans atomic bombs which killed millions of lives. The bomb was so huge that it was big enough to wipe out a whole city. Japan's morale was low and so were its people. People in Japan went as far as hating the Americans for causing such a human catastrophe. This was until Hellen came to visit Japan. Three years later after the atomic bomb was dropped on Japan, Hellen arrived and she was greeted by the Japanese people like a celebrity; 2 million people came out to welcome her. It was after this visit that Japan started to see the light and forgave America. Hellen worked tirelessly for individual freedom; even though being a socialist wasn't approved by everyone, she made the world a better place. In 1933, Hitler was made chancellor of Germany and so the Nazis were in power; they burnt many books that they saw as a threat, including Helen Keller's books. When Hellen first heard about it, she wrote an article in the *New York Times* where she said 'you can burn my books and the books of the best minds in Europe but the ideas have seeped through a million channels and will continue to quicken in other minds'. She didn't just fight for disabled people to live independently; she also fought for everyone by thinking outside the gap between the rich and the poor. By the early 1960s, Hellen suffered from strokes and stayed the remaining time at home in Connecticut but despite all this, she had won the hearts of the world; she had received lifetime awards in recognition for her achievements, including the Theodore Roosevelt distinguished service medal in 1936, the president medal of freedom in 1964 and election to the women's hall of fame in 1965. She received doctoral degrees from Temple University and Harvard University and from the universities of Glasgow, Scotland Berlin, Germany, Delhi, India, and Witwatersrand in Johannesburg, South Africa. Additionally, she was named an honorary fellow of the educational institute of Scotland.

Hellen sadly passed away in her sleep on 1 June 1968 just a few weeks before her 88th birthday. During her lifetime, she really set an example of determination, hard work, and imagination and the belief despite having a disability. Hellen is by far more than worthy of a place in this book.

Deafness Today

Throughout the world, most countries use both sign language and verbal teaching to teach the deaf. As dead people just want to be accepted in today's society, lip reading is more popular in America and across Europe because sign language can sometimes be seen as being dumb towards hearing people. People who are deaf never let the condition get in the way of living their lives as they rely on lip reading and sign language when needed. With the help of hearing aids, they can gain the hearing they long for but not all of deaf people gain access to them, hence the lip reading comes in handy. A deaf person has the capabilities like anyone else, to live like anyone else, just give them more time and patience to thrive and they will be ok; love is what they need.

Chapter XVIII
Blindness

Blindness is one of the oldest disabilities that we had as a human species; it dates back to when we were cave men and women. There's not really much information to say that an infection or an illness was the cause for our cavemen ancestors to turn blind but it's certainly most likely to be more natural causes; for example, bright lights in caves, the sun's light or when a tribe fights went horribly wrong and the eye would get hurt or damage by weaponry. We certainly know that our cavemen ancestors would've experienced blindness in some part of their lives; colour blindness also goes back to this time.

Ancient Egypt

In the ancient Egypt, there were a lot of myths and legends that surrounded blindness at this time. Egyptians had the belief that light, and fire were closely related to the sun and their God Ra which to them represented the source of life and wellbeing, and the dark meant danger and death which at night gave them the belief for fear. Egyptians believed that dreams were very powerful as dreams revealed an unknown world to give a glimpse into the future. Eyes were the most important organ in the body to the Egyptians along with the heart, of course. Eyes were important as they gave Egyptians a perception of the world around them. According to an Egyptian God called Horus, God of vision explains the role of each eye-one represents the moonlight which is dispersed into darkness of the night and the other represents the sunshine which creates life, combine the two together and both represents the power of the human intellect. Blindness however congenital or disease whatever the cause would've been was considered as a punishment. Anyone who had it would sink into a state of uncertainty and darkness. To protect the eyes, they would use eye drops and ointments which were believed to heal and chase away the insects and demons that threatened their vision. A variety of eye infections also existed around at this time. Egyptian eye doctors carried a special kit which contained green chrysocolla and black kohl makeup. Makeup played a massive role in Egyptian culture at this time;

even men wore it as they believed that it would protect them from demons. Make up was used as a prophylaxis (treatment for disease) and was also used to restore the brightness of divine glance and incite sun and moon to spread their beneficial light.

Blindness became more of a problem in ancient Egypt in the pyramid age because of sandstorms, Rabin heat, and dust from stones and buildings. These created hazardous conditions which contributed to blindness. They did have interesting ideas on treating it though; they thought eating powdered liver would cure night blindness. They also used a tortoise brain and performed a spell that would help but as time would tell, it did the opposite. As blindness in this time was considered as a form of punishment, blind people were seen very highly in Egyptian society. They would find it very hard to live as sometimes they would be left to die. If a blind person had a talent that was needed like a musician, for example, then they would pay him and the person could live by playing music to Pharos or people in the village.

Ancient Greece and Ancient Rome

Through the ancient world, blindness was seen in society as a divine punishment from the Gods. In Ancient Rome, many believed the individual was blinded due to eternal darkness which often left them thinking that they were cursed. Many blind people in this time struggled to live as there were very little ways of making money. Some were killed or left to starve. As time progressed to biblical times, blindness was thought to be caused by a sin against God. Society treated blind people pretty much the same until the thirteenth century when more was known, and people started speaking out and making life better for blind people. There was an event that happened in history which changed the lives of the blind for the better. After King Louis, the ninth of France lost a battle in the sixth crusade, he sustained bad injuries which left him feeling very restless. He returned to France with a newfound purpose in talking to people in his local communities and found a new interest in charities. He then helped to build the first institution for the blind which was not only the first of its kind in France but the first in the world. This institute enabled blind people to have the latest technology to learn and new methods to read and write. A new writing system was made to allow the blind to write for the first time, which involved pinpricks and silk onto cardboard. This was the start of a legacy for institutions to grow for the blind; this changed not only society but people's view of the blind because they could see that a blind person could be taught.

Schools for the Blind

The first school was founded by Valentin Haüy in Paris, France in 1784 which is known as the National Institute for the Young Blind. This was when people began to take an interest in teaching the blind which would become a massive step in improving the lives of the blind. Two years later, after he opened his school, King Louis, the ninth of France invited Valentin to show his skills in teaching the blind which was a success and in doing so, Valentin received enough funds to school 120 students. In 1791, a French Revolution started which left Valentin to move the school to another part of Paris as war was rife at this time. The school was combined with the capital's hospital and so the school, had another name change—the Institute of the Working Blind. In 1816, when the French Revolution was over, the school moved again; this time it was next to a former prison used in the French Revolution. Sebastian Guillié established the first ophthalmology clinic and became its director before being forced to leave in 1821 due to his brutality against his pupils. Although the previous location was worse than being a former prison, the lighting in the rooms were really badly lit the food wasn't very nice and the students were stinky as they were only allowed to take a bath once a month.

Louis Braille
4 January 1809–6
January 1852
The inventor of the
Braille System

Louis Braille is one the most important people in blind history who changed the way that blind people would communicate and learn forever.

Louis was born in France in a small town called Coupvray. He also had three older siblings Monique Catherine (1793), Louis-Simon (1795), and Marie Céline (1797) and lived with their parents, Simon-René and Monique. His father was a saddler where he'd repair saddles for horses in his workshop. Louis would spend a lot of time in his father's workshop; he loved holding his father's work tools in particular a hammer. When he was just three years old, his father asked him to put holes into a piece of leather but unfortunately things didn't go to plan as he was holding the piece of leather he raised his right hand with the hammer but sadly he hit his right eye which was an accident. His right eye was left infected from the wound and the infection passed onto his left eye causing blindness in both eyes. In 1821, Louis attended the Valentin's School for the blind in Paris. In one of Braille's first lessons, he learnt the communication system that the school had at the time. He also met Captain Charles Barbier who fought in the French army. Charles also invented night writing which was a code of dots and dashes onto thick paper which could be interpreted by the touch of a finger. This also proved useful on the battlefront as it was useful to communicate to other soldiers without the need to speak. The system was good but other people, including the blind and people who could see found it too complicated to understand. But the system inspired Louis to come up with his own writing system. Charles's system consisted of having 12 dots for each word. When Louis was only 15, he came up with an idea of using six dots rather than 12. What was remarkable was that he found 63 ways to use the 6-dot cell which wasn't any bigger than a fingertip.

By 1829, Louis had published his own form of communication for the blind which was named after him-the Braille System. Louis added new symbols and number so that Louis's system could be translated so that both sighted and the blind could read the same things which was revolutionary at the time. Louis also added symbols for mathematics and music which was useful for the blind so they could learn mathematics and music for the first time. By 1833, Louis was offered a full professorship where he taught geometry, history and algebra. Louis had a good ear for music which enabled him to play the organ and the cello. Between 1834 and 1839, Louis played the organ at two churches-one Church of Saint Nicolas des Champs and later, at the Church of Saint Vincent de Paul. Despite Louis's success, the public were sceptical about the Braille System. Even though Louis taught it at the Royal Institute, the Braille System wasn't out in the curriculum. This didn't stop blind people from learning it as blind people often taught themselves Braille at home or in secret. At the age of 40, Louis was forced to move back to his hometown of Coupvray. He had a persistent respiratory illness at the age of just 43; he died just two days after his birthday. It wasn't until 1854 that France officially adopted the Braille System as a way for the blind to read.

Legacy

Louis had provided blind people the power of communication through the Braille System. This was the first time that blind people had proper education which gave them the tools to become independent and to be who they wanted to be. Louis was a brilliant problem solver, a key mathematician and he used this knowledge to work out the symbols to use in his system.

Blind Education was still in its infancy across the world, but it was still growing rapidly in 1791. Seven years after France opened the first school for the blind, the first blind school in Britain was opened in Liverpool by a group of eight men; one was a blind musician called John Christie. William Ruscoe and Edward Rushtown were poets, writers who opposed slavery.

The Life of Edward Rushton

Edward Rushton
13 November 1756–22 November1814
British Poet
Who fought against the slave trade,
founded the first school for the blind in Britain

Like John & Christie, Edward was also blind but he had ophthalmia which resulted in inflamed eyes which was sadly left untreated. He got the illness while working as a sailor shipping slaves and cargo from Africa to the West Indies. At the age of 17, Edward saw first-hand on how slaves were treated on the ships; he sailed on but sadly sank to the bottom of the sea on a trip to New Guinea. These experiences made Edward to be in favour of abolishing the slave trade and allowing slaves to live free and prosperous lives. In 1773, the same year that his first ship sank, Edward went on another ship which set sail from Liverpool to Dominica but there was to be another tragedy as there was a dangerous disease which took hold of everyone on the ship ophthalmia (inflammation of the eye) which was highly contagious and struck many slaves and as it was often untreated, many people lost their sight. Appalled with the poor conditions the slaves were experiencing, Edward wanted to help them by providing food and water to help their morality. But it still didn't help their eye symptoms. As a consequence, for helping them, Edward got ophthalmia himself; he was completely blind in his left eye and slowly began to get cataracts in his right eye. He soon came back to Liverpool where he lived with his sister and was supported financially by his father who hired local boys to read to him. He started to learn about politics and philosophy. He had controversial views in politics where he criticised the British government in first poem called *The Dismembered Empire*. Edward even wrote to George Washington and Thomas Paine asking why they weren't using their public platform to stop and abolish slavery but neither of them replied.

Edward went on to marry Isabelle Rain in 1784. His father tried to run a tavern to earn some money and asked Edward to work alongside him. But Edward found it hard to keep up with the work, so he quit working with his father to write. He continued to write poems about his thoughts against the slave trade. His second poem, *The West Indian Eclogues* (short poem) explores more about Edward's first-hand experiences of the slaves and in general sea life. He later on became the editor of the *Liverpool Herald* which was the local newspaper at the time. But it was short lived as he refused to change his views on the slave trade. Edwards books started to sell by this time and he became an established author. He began to live comfortably on his wealth, and he could also afford to pay for his children's education. In the late 1780s, he became a member of the literary and philosophical society. Soon after, Edward donated a lot of money to poor blind people who were in serious need. This led Edward to set up a school for the blind which was called the Liverpool School for the Indigent Blind. Since then, it's had a name change to the Royal School for the Blind in Liverpool. In 1803, Edward had an operation on his eyes so that he could see for the first time in 33 years. He could see his wife Isabelle and children. In 1811, his wife passed away along with one of his daughters; Edward died three years later of paralysis.

With an everlasting legacy that still exists today in building the first blind school in Britain, Edward also became the first blind person to build a school which was an achievement in itself. To some, he may be controversial but behind his opinions was the need to change things for the better for the blind. Back to the school-at the start of its history, it was uncertain because the first venue wasn't suitable to be a school; money wasn't available so they relied on charitable donations from the public and the student welfare wasn't up to high standards with not very nice food.

By the 1800s, enough money was raised from donations and John Foster (architect) was hired which was the start to build a proper school close by on London road. The school gained a good reputation throughout the years and would stay here for the next 50 years. In 1806, the school had a royal visit from the Prince of Wales, Later, on his visit, become King George IV met with Edward, John and William who founded the school and showed him around the school and what they did for blind people in the community. George had admired their work. They showed George their manufactured goods that were available and was entertained by the school choir. They all sang the chorus of Hallelujah. George liked all this very much; he ordered that each pupil be given 10 Guineas; the prince also gave the school money as well- 100 Guineas. He didn't stop there; he authorised them to have the royal patronage which continues to support the school even today. After the royal visit, more plans were made to improve the school. John Foster was hired again but this time, he focused on expanding the back of the school which created new facilities and consisted of work rooms, technical rooms and music rooms which were all completed by 1812. For the first time, the school didn't feel like an asylum; it felt cosier and was designed to give blind people comfort. As Lime Street Station was expanding because of the popularity of trains, it was putting pressure on the teachers to keep the school running in the area, so the school was forced to move location from Hope Street to Hardman Street in 1851. The new school still had the chapel next to the school and it was big enough to teach 85 pupils which was big at the time. In 1893, the new elementary education system was out in place to ensure that all children would get the best education they could. However, The Hardman Blind School wasn't meeting the requirements that the new education system had set out; therefore, it lost its place and a new plot of land was bought in Waver Street providing education to 5–16-year-olds and at the age of 16, they had the choice to be transferred back to Hardman School for the blind for technical lessons.

Blind Education in America

The first school for the blind in America was established in 1829; it was called the New England Sulus for the Blind. Today, the New England Asylum is called the Perkins School for the Blind in Watertown, Massachusetts. In New York, a school was founded in 1831. In 1832, an institution for the education of the blind. Now called the Overbrook school for the blind was founded in Philadelphia. At first, schools for the blind were solely used to provide blind students skills for employment once they become adults. They taught the blind what was known as the 'blind trades'-chair caning, basket weaving, rug weaving etc. so that they could find work and live independently. However, this plan had failed, the blind were not able to find work as they couldn't support themselves.

In 1850, the first sheltered shop was created for blind workers in New York. This shop was simply used for the blind trades which a lot of people used. The American Printing house for the blind (APH) was founded in Louisville, Kentucky. In 1879, APH was made the official printer of schoolbooks for blind students in America. The American Association of instructors of the blind was created in 1871 which was the first organisation for blind teachers in America; this was so that the teachers in the community could come together and discuss any problems or things that were happening throughout local schools. In the beginning of the twentieth century, the American Association of Workers for the Blind was created in 1905. It consisted primarily of protecting the rights for blind workers in the management of the sheltered shops. Eventually, other blind workers in different jobs particularly who were involved in rehabilitation programs joined the American Association of Workers in America. In 1918, Braille was accepted as the standard way of teaching the blind in America. In 1921, the American Foundation for the Blind was created by the American Association of Instructors and the American Association of Workers for the blind. These two organisations got together in a meeting in Vinton, Iowa. They believed by combining and working together, the lives for the blind could be enhanced greatly. There were four original purposes to conduct research into the causes of blindness-work together to find the resources that to help improve the lives of the blind, improve services for the blind; and to represent the interests of the blind.

What Causes Blindness?

Well, in order to answer this, we need to find out the types of blindness as there are many to explore. Let's start with one of the more common ones that affects the elderly. Cataracts can make your vision very cloudy. The patient may have blurry or misty vision. The cataracts lie in between the lens and the pupil of the eye. Surgery is the only way to remove it. Colour blindness is very rare and more common in men than women because men have a Y chromosome and women have both X chromosomes that they are less likely to gain gene defects. It is suggested that 8 per cent of men have colour blindness whereas for women it's only 0.5%. Colour blindness essentially is a gene defect that affects the way that we see colour red and green. Colour blindness is passed on from the mother to the son. It can also be causes by eye disease, age and retina damage.

Diabetic Macular Oedema (DME)

This type is the leading cause of blindness for people who have diabetes; it can occur in type 1 and 2 diabetes which may develop diabetic retinopathy or damage the small blood cells inside the retina which helps us to see objects in front of us. The patient may experience swelling in the eye as well. The primary risk to DME is high blood sugar levels, high blood pressure and high cholesterol which will also cause blindness and make the symptoms of DME worse.

DME is monitored through the newest and latest technology as it makes it easier for doctors to find it. Before the technology, they would notice the swelling in the eye but not necessarily know how much swelling and how effective different treatments could be. There are many treatments for DME is but the common way is to make sure that the blood sugar levels go down; this not only improves the symptoms of DME but also diabetes. Your blood sugar levels will be monitored on a three-month basis to make sure that the sugar levels are on track. The doctor may suggest eye treatments such as laser eye surgery which stops the leakage of the small blood vessels (capillaries) in the eye. Eye injections are available to stop the growth and leakage of the blood vessels, but the patient may have them for many years.

Dry eyes can cause blindness as they aren't producing the tears which helps lubricate the eyes to stop irritation and vision problems. It can be caused by disease, age and structure of the eye. The symptoms include itching of the eye, pain, blurry vision and red eyes. Different people are affected differently. Luckily, these symptoms are easily treatable by seeing a doctor or using prescriptive eye drops.

Glaucoma

This is an eye disease which damages the optic nerve which leads to loss of vision and total blindness if left untreated. Glaucoma usually affects both eyes and it is the second leading cause of blindness. Glaucoma also is divided into two categories where you have open angled Glaucoma (OAG) and narrow angled Glaucoma (NAG). Treatments are eye drops through lasers, also surgeries can be done to treat it.

Hyperopia

Also known as farsightedness, it's a common refractive error in which close objects to the patient seem blurry and far away objects are seen more clearly. The condition forces the eye to focus on images behind the retina rather than on the retina. Symptoms include blurry vision, headaches or eye strain; treatments include wearing glasses or contact lenses. For more serious cases, laser surgery is used as treating it.

Macular Degeneration

Also known as age-related macular degeneration (AMD); this condition is the degeneration of the macula which is the light sensitive area at the back of the eye. The macula is responsible for central vision (straight ahead vision); it's one of the leading causes of vision loss and blindness. Treatments include having a healthy diet and exercising making sure that you have the right vitamins and minerals daily.

Myopia

It is also known as near-sightedness and short-sightedness; this condition makes the patient not being able to focus their vision on far away objects making them appear blurry. Myopia is thought to be caused by genetics and the environment. Common symptoms of myopia are squinting the eyes, eye strain and headaches.

Optic Neuritis

This condition is caused by inflammation or demyelination of the optic nerve which transmits the image from the retina to the brain. Optic neuritis causes vision loss which differs depending on the severity of the patient's symptoms; the good thing about optic neuritis is that it doesn't always need treatment as it can heal by itself but medication such as corticosteroids can help speed recovery.

Pink Eye (Conjunctivitis)

This is when the conjunctiva which is between the eyelid and the eye is inflamed. It is also the membrane that covers the white area of the eye. It can make the eye appear pink or reddish in colour, it can also have yellow puss that surrounds the eye. It is caused by virus, bacteria and allergies. With regards to treating conjunctivitis, the bacterial one can be treated by antibacterial eye drops. Conjunctivitis is most popular among babies and little children. Adults can get it but it is less likely to happen.

Presbyopia

This type of blindness is one of the more common ones which affects the elderly which leaves the vision being very blurry. Often, presbyopia can make it hard for the patient to focus on an object, reading using a computer, or a smartphone. As this condition comes with age, there is no way to reverse it; you'd have to stop the ageing process. However, there are ways of helping the symptoms which involves wearing glasses or contact lenses. Or if you want to you can have laser eye surgery.

Strabismus

This type is also known as cross eye because one eye looks a different way than the other eye. Most cases are caused by poor neuromuscular control of the eyes. This is when the link between the eyes and the brain can't get the messages to control the eyes; eye injuries can cause it. There are two different types of Strabismus/

Intermittent exotropia-This type of strabismus occurs when an eye or eyes tends to point beyond the object being viewed due to an inability to coordinate both eyes. Side effects of intermittent exotropia are eye strain, difficulty reading, headaches, and difficulty with vision in bright sunlight.

Accommodative exotropia-This type of strabismus occurs because of uncorrected farsightedness; the extra strain needed to keep eyes focused may cause the eyes to turn inward. Symptoms may include double vision, closing or covering one eye when reading or doing other close work, and tilting or turning of the head in an effort to focus properly.

Treating strabismus requires a number of options-wearing glasses or contact lenses, patching the good eye, prism lenses help change the light that enter the eye which helps to reduce the amount of turning the eye has to do to focus. Vision therapy which provides some exercises which are designed to help coordination and the ability of eyes to focus.

Lastly surgery, where the surgeon will try to tighten or loosen to correct the alignment so that both eyes match. After the preceding, you may need to have eye drops (with or without corticosteroids) with an eye patch as part of the medical procedure.

Is Blindness Genetic?

There approximately 350 different eye diseases that can be genetically passed on from one or both of our parents who already experience blindness. These conditions are known as albinism, aniridia, colour blindness, corneal dystrophies, glaucoma, keratoconus, leber congenital amaurosis, night blindness, retinitis pigmentosa and retinoblastoma. The most common way of how the genetic mutation form in blindness works through monogenic gene disorders which falls into two categories-the first one is when the gene mutation is present in the person's DNA. The gene mutation that causes blindness only needs to be copied once to cause blindness. The second type is based on more than one mutation that's found inside the genome.

The Findings of the MARK3 Gene Mutation

A study was put together to research families that had more than one mutated gene in their genome and the research was conducted on 200 families from Pakistan. They restarted by looking into the genomes of every family member. One family in particular had three children who had more than one gene mutations and two children who were perfectly healthy. They wanted to find if there was more than one copy of the gene mutation in the affected three children and one or none in the healthy siblings. After the research was done and the results came in, an interesting discovery had been found-an unknown disorder had been found which led to the cause of children being born blind. Having searched further into the disorder, they found that it was a new gene which was mutated. This was a breakthrough in blindness and genetics. They named the gene MARK3; to confirm that it was the MARK3 gene scientists had looked into a similar mutation in drosophilae (a species of a round worm) which had affected the round worms with blindness the same way as humans experienced it. The gene mutation doesn't allow the eye to grow properly while in the womb. They also conducted a test where they had two copies of MARK3 gene on a swarm of flies and the eyes of the flies didn't grow properly leaving them blind which was similar to the families in Pakistan. The MARK3 gene is located in chromosome 4 right at the bottom with reference numbers 32.32 and 32.33

Blindness Today

Similar to deaf people, the blind rely on the company of people, or the kindness of friends and family to gain independence. With additional support in school supply teachers. The kindness of strangers after they leave school. A blind person can still live life as a normal person; like with the deaf, you've just got to give them more time and let the flourish on their own merit. The one thing that we all need to bear in mind is the only real disability that we can all have is the limits we put on ourselves. Blindness is no exception; the blind can dream, can do anything they want like anyone else; just let them lead the way and they'll show you.

Chapter XIX
Huntington's Disease

The very first stories of Huntington's date back to medieval times. At the time, it wasn't called Huntington's; it was called Chorea which dates back to the Middle Ages where there was very little knowledge on disability. Chorea comes from the Greek and Latin word chorus or a group of dances; reason being that people at this time thought that they had a dancing disorder which wasn't the case. In fact, it was their way of explaining the muscle jerk movements or twitching as one of the symptoms of Huntington's. It may or may not surprise you that people at this time thought they were cursed by the devil and were told to keep an eye on them or they were to be sent to their death through execution. There's a story of a witch who was alive in the 1690s in Salem, Massachusetts. She was thought to have Huntington's and therefore executed. Throughout the eighteenth and nineteenth, century very little was known about chorea, it was a disease that was killing people quite quickly which gave doctors or people who wanted to help them very little time as life expectancy was very short in those days. As time passed, life expectancy grew which gave modern doctors more time to find out what chorea really was and to learn about its symptoms. It wasn't until the twentieth century where progress was made, and scientist found the gene that was causing the condition.

What is Huntington's Disease?

Huntington's is a progressive brain disorder which causes uncontrollable movements, emotional problem and memory loss. Huntington's is at its most common when the patient is in 30s or 40s; the first signs before diagnosis may include depression, irritability, poor coordination, inability of making decisions and trouble learning new information. After the diagnosis is confirmed, the common symptoms the patient will experience are muscle jerking or twitching. As the disorder progresses, the twitching becomes worse and may also affect walking, talking, and swallowing. People with Huntington's may experience difference in personality, decline in thinking, decision making and reasoning abilities. People who have Huntington's expect to live for about 15 to 20 years after they get the first symptoms. There is another form of Huntington's which is less common which affects children or teenagers. It is called juvenile Huntington's which also involves mobility and emotional changes. There are other problems as well such as clumsiness, slowness in movement, fainting or falling, slurred speech and drooling. When it comes to school and performance in school, students who have Huntington's will struggle to keep up with the rest of the class. Their reasoning abilities can become impaired and 30–50% of student have epileptic seizures with Huntington's. It is certainly a battle ground. Children and teenagers who have Huntington's don't expect to live as long as an adult; only 15–20 years max after symptoms arise.

The Genetics of Huntington's Disease

The main causes of Huntington's Disease are from a gene mutation which is called the HTT gene which is a gene mutation. The HTT gene helps build a protein called Huntingtin, the role that it plays is still unknown, but it seems to play a very important role when it comes to the nerve cells in the brain. The HTT gene mutation involves a DNA segment which is made up of three building blocks (cytosine, adenine, and guanine). These three building blocks are repeated 10 to 35 times in a gene; this happens for people who don't have HD; for people that do have HD, the building blocks are repeated more than 36 to 120 times. Bearing in mind people with 36–39 repeats may or may not have the symptoms of Huntington's but any more than 40 will cause the symptoms of Huntington's. What also happens, the more times the building blocks are repeated, the huntingtin protein gets longer, eventually the longer protein gets cut into smaller toxic fragments which bind together and accumulate in the neurons which disrupts the normal function of the neuron cells which eventually leads to the death of normal function brain cells. This is the start of the symptoms of Huntington's Disease.

Inheriting Huntington's Disease

One thing to keep in mind is that Huntington's is an autosomal dominant disorder which means only one copy of HTT from either your mother or father is enough to inherit the condition. But on rarer occasions, with no family history of Huntington's Disease, children can still get Huntington's which starts when the HTT gene newly develops in the child's DNA. When somebody has inherited Huntington's from either parent, the number of CAG trinucleotide repeats in the HTT gene which gives the child a larger amount of the repeats which leads to the patient having the symptoms of Huntington's earlier in life. Adults who have Huntington's Disease usually have 40–50 repeats while juvenile HD which occurs in children or teenagers has about 60 or more repeats in the HTT gene. Which is rare, but does happen.

Who Discovered Huntington's Disease?

George Huntington (9 April 1850–3 March 1916) (Founder of Huntington's Disease)

George Huntington was born on 9 April 1850 in East Hampton, Long Island, America. His family were wealthy as both his father and grandfather were also physicians. George was the third generation in his family to be a physician. His grandfather started the tradition Abel Huntington (1778–1858) and his father followed George Lee Huntington (1811–1881); all three members shared their own family practice; they all had passion for observing people with mysterious diseases. George's father and his grandfather played a vital role in helping George find the symptoms for Huntington's Disease. His grandfather Abel graduated at Clinton Academy in his native town and in 1868, he began his medical studies at the College of Physicians and Surgeons at Columbia University in New York. In 1871, George made real progress as he was the first member in the family to write the first symptoms of chorea as it was known at this time. At the age of 22, George found that chorea was an inherited disease passed on from parents.

In Philadelphia on 13 April 1872, he published his first paper on the condition. He wrote 'chorea is essentially a disease of the nervous system; the name chorea is given to the disease on the account of the slowing properties of those affected by it. Which certainly describes the progressive slowing down of movement and progressive decay of the body'. One year after completing his medical graduation with very little clinical experience, he gave his first speech on chorea. In his speech, he pointed out the characteristics of chorea, but mostly he talked about the symptoms of Sydenham's disease. It was only late into the speech that he went in detail of the type of chorea that was named after him. He

166

knew that that it was an inherited disease that adults could get; he pointed out slow and progressive nature of the disease.

In 1872, the same year that George's paper on chorea was published, the German medical press took an interest in George's findings so much so that they introduced it to the European medical literature which increased recognition of the disease throughout Europe. Amazingly, the description that George spoke about chorea wasn't changed or adapted by any other physician of this time. In fact, several years later in 1887, chorea started to be renamed as Huntington's Chorea. But despite the success in Europe, George didn't have any patients in Rhode Island with the disease. This success would've been impossible without his father's and grandfather's files to which he never denied the dedication that his family did. Both of his ancestors wrote down their findings which created huge files. The files contained generations of people who were suffering with chorea.

George studied and analysed his father's notes. George had memories as a young boy of his father taking him to East Hampton to see the sick as his father was there to try and help them feel better. His father wrote about the gradual mental breakdown as the motor neurones deteriorated which George also saw as a child which left an ever-lasting impact on George. From that moment, he knew that he wanted to follow in his father's footsteps into helping people suffering from chorea. Despite having a successful start to his career, he chose to be a general practitioner just like his father was. He just wanted to have a simple life as a general practitioner. Not having the stress of academic life certainly gave him a bit more freedom in what he wanted to do in his future. In 1874, George married his long-term girlfriend Mary Elizabeth Hackard from Pomeroy. The young couple returned to George's hometown in East Hampton. George tried to run his own medical practice; a few months later the young couple moved to New York. George went back to what he knew best and was a successful physician and he worked until 1901. George led a very happy life in the countryside when he wasn't working; he enjoyed his hobbies in drawing wildlife and going fishing. He also liked music and played the flute along with his wife who liked playing the piano.

Mary and George had five children who he adored very much; from early ages, he taught them to learn and work hard in life which stayed with them for the rest if their lives. George's second child Edwin Huntington also chose like his father to be a doctor which made him the fourth generation in a row to become one in the family.

Towards the end of George's life, he was suffering from bad asthma attacks. In a bid to try and get better, he moved from New York to North Carolina; he had a two-year convalescence (recovery process). He managed to feel better and he returned to New York in 1903 in Hopewell which was close to where he used to live in LaGrangeville. He went back to his practice again and for some time served as a visiting physician at Matteawan Hospital. He also visited a village called Fish Kill in Dutchess, New York. George never complained about the lack of patients; however, the patients that he treated were often poor and couldn't afford their medical bills. George never refused to treat someone who couldn't afford his services because he knew that it was the right thing to do. George continued to work hard until 1915 until his health deteriorated once again. Towards the end of 1915 and the beginning of 1916, George wasn't well; he suffered with breathing and coughing problems. On 3 March 1916, he died of pneumonia aged 66; he died in his son's Edwin's home in Cairo, New York.

George's Legacy

In 1908, a fellow physician William Osler reviewed his paper and he said that in the history of medicine, there have been very few instances where a disease has been more accurately, more graphically or more briefly described.

I find it a fitting tribute that chorea as it was once known was renamed after George because not only was it honouring him but also it was honouring his father and grandfather for the hard work as physicians. I'm sure that George would agree with that.

Huntington's Disease Today

Huntington's isn't cured yet but it's a condition that's well managed with medication and therapies to help manage the symptoms. It's estimated that between 10,000 and 30,000 people have Huntington's in the United States; juvenile Huntington's just covers 16% of the population that suffer from Huntington's. Throughout Europe, the numbers are similar to American stats; 5–10 per 100,000 in Africa and Asia Huntington's is considerably lower at 1 per 100,000 people suffer with it. No one knows what makes the numbers go up or down; whether it's lifestyle or the different country you live in. But I'm the future; I'm hopeful that Huntington's will become a distant memory as science is making breakthrough every day. People will be able to live their lives without it and be free from Huntington's forever.

Chapter XX
Locked-In Syndrome

Locked in Syndrome (LIS) also known as (pseudo coma) is a rare neurological disorder where the whole body is paralysed from head to toe. It is also common to get the condition confused with motor neurone disease as both patients are wheelchair bound and they can't move their bodies. However, there a few differences in that in Locked in Syndrome the body is paralysed a lot sooner as compared to MND as it slowly progresses over time. The only area of the body which can move is the eyes and that is why patients rely on computers to help them communicate better. In the nineteenth century, a book was published by Alexandre Dumas; he titled it *The Count of Monte Cristo*. Alexandre wrote, 'Sight and hearing were the only senses remaining. However by one of his senses could help him reveal the thoughts and feelings that still occupied his mind and the look by which he gave an expression to his inner life, was like the distant gleam of a candle which a traveller sees by night across some desert place and knows that the living dwells beyond the silence of obscurity. So, although the movement of the arm, the sound of the voice, and the agility of the body, were wanting, the speaking eye sufficed for all'. I think this description describes Locked in Syndrome beautifully; the symptoms of what the patients goes through but also shows that sometimes, you don't need movement or a voice to communicate with people and sight is all you need to cover the use of all three senses of the body. It also happens to be the only description of LIS at this time and as there is no record of any physician to have discovered LIS, you could say that Alexandre discovered the condition himself. There is more than meets the eye about LIS as it's so rare that it can be difficult in diagnosing.

The Types of Locked-In Syndrome

There are three 3 types which fall into categories where you have the classic (type 1) which is caused by quadriplegia and anarthria which has preserved consciousness and vertical eye movements. Then there's the incomplete category (type 2) which is the same as the first type, but the difference is voluntary movement and vertical eye movements. The final type is the most severe out of the three. Total category where the whole body is paralysed and the patient doesn't have the ability to speak; the only thing that functions properly is the eyes.

The Causes of Locked-In Syndrome

The main cause for LIS is damage to specific part of the brain stem which is the piece of the brain that goes down towards the top of the spinal cord. This is known as the pons. Now, the pons contain important neuronal pathways between the cerebrum, spinal cord and cerebellum. When a patient has LIS, there's interruption of all motor functions as they stop working which leads to full paralysis. Further damage to the brain stem affects the face muscles and the ability to talk. A brain haemorrhage is when the ventral pons in the brain stem is dead which then leads to heavy bleeding in or outside of the brain or there can be lack of blood going to the brain which is called infarct haemorrhage which leads to a brain haemorrhage. There additional causes to LIS which include infection in certain portions of the brain, tumours, loss of protective insulation myelin that surrounds the nerve cells, myelinolysis or inflammation of the nerves, polymyositis and finally ALS which more commonly known as being associated with motor neurone disease. While having LIS, the patient loses the ability to breathe, talk, chew, swallow and move on their own to which they need help. The life expectancy is ten years after the first symptoms of LIS arise in rare cases though patients make some recovery in movement but not fully. But even on rarer occasions, people make a full recovery. So, there is hope but doesn't always happen.

Treatment

Treating LIS: There isn't a guaranteed cure for LIS; however, there are different ways of managing the condition. People with LIS find it difficult to breathe and eat on their own, so they will need assistance from a ventilator to breathe for them and a feeding tube that's inverted into the stomach so that they are getting the right amount of nutrients they need to survive. Also, a whole range of therapists are there to help ease the symptoms. Physical therapy is on hand to help make them feel more comfortable and they help to prevent systemic complications such as respiratory infections. Speech therapists are on hand to help people with LIS communicate better with the people around them as the only thing that can move is their eyes and a speech therapist will help the patient communicate better through eye movements and blinking. Electronic communication devices help a lot with their communication; devices such as infrared eye movement sensors and computer voice prosthetics are allowing people with LIS to have a voice and speak more freely and have access to the internet. Motorised wheelchairs have increased independence and continue to do so for people with LIS.

Who Discovered Locked-In Syndrome?

Fred was born on 10 January 1924 in Atlantic City in New Jersey. His father was Frederick Plum and he was a chemist and he owned a small chain of drug stores. During this time, it was in the result of the Great American Depression and he had no choice but to sell all of them. When Fred was a teenager, he found new motivation to become a neurologist as his sister Christine passed away from polio. In 1944, Fred graduated at Dartmouth college where he earned his medical degree from Cornell in 1947. Later that year, he published his first scientific paper in biochemistry with Dr Vincent du Vigneaud, later he won his first Nobel Prize. When war broke out in Korea in 1950, Dr Plum worked in the United States Naval Hospital in St Albans Queens. Three years later, aged 29, Fred became the head of neurology in Washington University in Seattle; he was one of the youngest neurologists to take the top job at this time. It was here the Dr Plum started his own respiratory centre mainly because people who were paralysed or unconscious would eventually lose the ability to breathe. Shortly after, there was an outbreak of polio which swept through Alaska. Dr Plum flew to Alaska as soon as he heard the news. In doing so, he helped the local doctors use the iron lungs machine so that patients could get help to breathe. The Seattle Centre also treated people who were in a coma which was due to drug overdose. At this time, doctors solely relied on bedside clinical examination because there was no MRI scans or CT scan, not even ultrasound. This made diagnosing a patient more challenging, but it didn't mean that they weren't diagnosed, just

Fred Plum (10 January 1924– 11 June 2010) American Neurologist who discovered Locked in Syndrome

more likely to not being diagnosed correctly. Regarding brain injuries, there were only a few things that doctors knew that contributed to being in a coma: swelling of the brain, degenerative brain diseases, impaired consciousness and brain death. Doctors could only treat a few of these conditions as the knowledge wasn't as good as it is today.

In seeking more knowledge in consciousness, Dr Plum and his team conducted more tests in analysing metabolism, cerebrospinal fluid, and the flow of blood through the blood vessels. In one experiment, Dr Plum, Dr Posner and Dr Raichle breathed in and out very fast for five hours to see how hyperventilation affected the brain. They found that blood circulation to the brain became limited as breathing was quickening, both oxygen and carbon dioxide levels being low led to the blood vessels in the brain to become thin which meant less blood entered the brain. This also taught doctors to be careful when hyperventilating while treating a patient who had brain damage as this would cause more pressure on the brain due to long periods of hyperventilation.

In the early 1970s, Dr Plum teamed up with a Scottish Neurosurgeon Dr William Bryan Jennett. Dr Jennett came up with a reliable way of measuring somebody's consciousness; he called it the Glasgow coma scale. A person was assessed according to the scale. The severity of a patient's consciousness was between 1 and 6;1 being the worst and 6 closest to normal. It measured eye, motor and verbal function. Doctors still use this scale today as it remains the golden standard to measure consciousness in LIS. To put it into better detail.

Eye response which ranges from 1 to 3

Motor response which ranges between 1 and 6

Verbal response which ranges between 1 and 5

While looking at the eyes, 1 on the scale meant that the eyes couldn't open; 2 meant the eyes could open but only in response to pain; 3 meant eyes open when listening to someone talking. There were 6 grades to measure the severity of motor skills the patient had: 1 was no motor movement at all, 2 a reaction to the pain. What I mean by that is the upper limbs can change to look more rigid which may explain the pain levels that the person is going through. The third grade meant body was locked in with different posture known as decorticate where the arms were on the chest and the legs were straight but rotated inwards. In the fourth grade, body was unable to move due to pain in the limbs, fifth grade allowed body to move but with pain and the final sixth grade meant that people could move normally without a problem. And finally, this brings us to monitoring verbal skills which range 1 to 5: number 1 meant that they were unable to speak; 2 on the scale meant you could understand what they are saying and 3 if they were moaning or groaning or even swearing, then you put them down as talking words; 4 if they were disorientated, then they were marked as confused; 5 on the scale meant that they could speak normally.

In the late 1970s, Dr Plum often used the term 'persistent vegetative state' which is his way of explaining LIS and that's how the condition is more commonly known today. Dr Plum was a true believer in putting the patient first by giving them the best treatments that he could give but if he and his team couldn't save a patient after trying their best in looking after a patient, then he would except putting them to sleep as a last resort. In 1994, Dr Plum treated President Nixon during the late stages of his life; he suffered a stroke under Fred's care; he was improving as he released a public statement. But then later on after his health got worse again and Fred had discussed the best possible treatment plans for him, the president died on 22 April 1994 as a result of the stroke that caused swelling of the brain which caused a deep coma which killed him.

Personal Life

Dr Plum married a woman called Jean Houston; they had three children together-a daughter called Carol and a son called Christopher and the other called Michael. They had a really long and happy marriage until it sadly ended in divorce. Jean died in 1999 but Fred lived on and married for the second time to Susan Plum. Towards the end of Fred's life, he was developing symptoms that were similar to dementia and he died on 11 June 2010 due to Alzheimer's Disease.

Legacy

What a legacy Fred has left us with his pioneering neurological research. He was able to successfully diagnose patients with LIS even though he didn't have the MRI and CT scans we take for granted today. His team also allowed doctors to find a way of improving the quality of life for people with Locked in Syndrome. As a fitting tribute to Dr Fred Plum, I thought I'd share some fitting words which perfectly describe his medical career and the principles that he stood for throughout his life. 'His passionate belief in the right of an individual to define his own quality of life and to die with dignity allowed him to see the treatment choices from the view of the patient, rather than as simply a challenge for the physician'. (Susan Plum)

Locked-In Syndrome Today

Today, both men and women can equally get LIS; even children can get it. Patients are most at risk after a brain tumour or after being in a coma for a long time. It is not yet known roughly how many patients suffer with Locked in Syndrome worldwide. But in the UK, there are roughly 9,000 patients that suffer from a brain tumour each year, from children to adults. A brain tumour doesn't guarantee that you'll get LIS, but the chances get higher as the tumour forces the brain to lose its functions for a small amount of time. People with LIS have to rely on everyone around them to live life as closest to normal as possible as they can't do anything by themselves. It's hard to say to say if LIS will have a cure in the near future but in the long term, when we study stem cells as they can help repair brain cells, this will be the start to getting closer to finding a cure. As the brain needs to be repaired from the tumour or in general in order for the patient to get bet better and gain movement in their body. As I said earlier, I believe that the brain can heal itself it just needs the right cells to do so.

Chapter XXI
Scoliosis

Scoliosis is a condition where the spine is curved sideways which affects the posture; the curvature looks like a C shape or in severe cases, the spine is shaped as an S. Symptoms may start reasonably well but gradually get worse over time. Scoliosis also has two other types to consider which are called Lordosis and Kyphosis which can also cause other health problems which include:

Back Pain, shoulders, neck and buttock Pain nearest the bottom of the back.

Respiratory or cardiac problems in (severe cases).

Constipation due to curvature causing 'tightening' of stomach, intestines, etc.

Limited mobility secondary to pain or functional limitation in adults.

Painful menstruation.

Other signs of scoliosis can include:

Uneven musculature on one side of the spine.

Rib prominence or a prominent shoulder blade, caused by rotation of the rib cage in thoracic scoliosis.

Uneven hips, arms, or leg lengths, even shoulder heights.

Slow nerve action.

Heart and lung problems in (severe cases)

Calcium deposits in the cartilage endplate and sometimes in the disc itself.

The C curvature has three types which determines the area of the back in which it has the most impact.

The Thoracic Curve

Also known as lordosis, the thoracic curve affects the top of the spine which is located between the cervical nerves (at the top of the spine) and the lumbar region (bottom of spine); this leaves the spine curving inwards instead of being straight. There are a number of reasons that causes lordosis. First osteoporosis which leaves the bones to become weak and fragile and causes the bones to compress and fracture which then leads to spinal deformities. The second reason is when the patient has a misaligned vertebra which means that the disks in between the bones have too much pressure which results in degeneration of the disks and bones which causes the spine to curve. A third cause is spondylolisthesis where a disk slips out of its normal position. The fourth reason include conditions like Elhers Danlos Syndrome and Marfan Syndrome where bones with connective tissues over grow which causes instability in the spine. The fifth reason is obesity that can cause curvature by an imbalance in weight causing spine to deform. Yet another cause is inflammation of the intervertebral discs which is caused by sports injuries or lifting heavy objects the wrong way.

Thoracolumbar Scoliosis

Is an abnormal curvature of the spine which is in the middle of the back. This is where the spine curves towards the right although it can curve to the left but that's rare. It is more common in women to experience; men can also suffer from this problem. It can be caused by a birth defect where the spine will curve in the womb similar to spina bifida; it can also be caused by muscle weakness or poor muscle control. Treatments depend on how bad the curve is; if the cure isn't severe and not progressing, then there is no need for treatment. However, if the curvature is progressing or it's naturally severe, then surgery is needed to correct the spine. If the curve is cause by weak muscles, then an exercise routine can help strengthen the muscles to help the spine.

The Lumbar Curve

Which affects the bottom of the spine; in severe cases, it combines with the thoracic curve going in one direction and the lumbar going the opposite way. Treating the lumbar curve depends on a number of factors, including age, overall health of the patient, to the severity of the curve. If the patient experiences any pain symptoms or inflammation, then the doctor would prescribe some ibuprofen or other pain relief to reduce the discomfort. If the pain is still present or gets worse, then your doctor would recommend corticosteroid injections in the spine to reduce inflammation. These injections are performed under an X-ray. The patient can only receive no more than four injections in the span of 6–12 months. If the curve gets worse (progresses), then the only option at this point is surgery; the patient will need it as it will affect general wellbeing in the long run. The surgery is called spinal fusion which involves metal rods and inserting them into the spine and securing them with screws. Like with most surgeries, it does have side effects which do tend to put some people off.

Kyphosis

This is where the spine curves outwards and it causes the patient to look like they are bending over while they stand or walk. This condition is also known as round back; it has been seen popularly in old ladies or witches. Kyphosis affects mainly the thoracic spine which is in the centre. Kyphosis is measured between 20–45 degrees if the patient has a measurement less than 20 degrees is close to normal and shouldn't affect mobility but anything more than 45 degrees is quite severe; anything above 50 degrees is what's called hyper kyphosis which affects mobility and may need medical attention. Kyphosis can affect people of all ages, but it affects teenagers going through puberty more commonly. In most cases of Kyphosis, it causes little harm to health but may need additional support using a brace or using exercise to strengthen the muscles to improve the patient's posture and strengthen the spine. In severe cases which may lead to health problems such as breathing problems and doctors may recommend a surgery to straighten the spine using metal rods and to improve their symptoms in the long term.

AIS (Adolescent Idiopathic Scoliosis)

The final type which affects children in the late stages of their childhood or young teenage years while the body is going through a growth spurt and that is Adolescent Idiopathic Scoliosis (AIS). This occurs because as the body is growing, the spine grows the wrong way and therefore, curves; hence the idiopathic bit. This condition progresses over time meaning it'll get worse without doing anything to treat it. However, mild curvature of the spine is equally common in both boys and girls because it happens as the body grows. The cause for AIS is unknown; however, there are clues going back hundreds of thousands of years and involves looking into our genetics and the environmental factors that played a role in the cause. This suggests a range of problems, hormonal problems, abnormal muscle and bone growth and problems with our nervous system that may be the causes. Some researchers say that some genes cause AIS; other genes determines how severe. However, many of these genes have been researched and tested and there isn't a clear answer into which genes are responsible for the problem. In regard to inheritance from your family, AIS mainly affects people in families that don't have history of the condition or the condition can cluster in the family, meaning it can skip two or three generations which makes the inheritance patterns very unclear as there are so many genetic and environmental factors which play their part; however, what is clear is if a close relative (father mother brother or sister) has the condition, then it makes the individual more likely to suffer with AIS.

The History of Scoliosis

The beginning of scoliosis is quite similar to where you'd find out osteoporosis or osteogenesis imperfecta when humans lived in caves. During an unpredicted event which span across the whole of northern western Europe, a devastating ice age came which certainly left its impact on the environment and us. Like I said before about the events that started osteogenesis imperfecta, scoliosis started the same way where the ice age decreased the sun's energy from the cold air and the thick clouds which left us with not much calcium which is essential for healthy bones. Our ancestors didn't have the right amount of nutrients for our bones to survive which left scoliosis to develop. The ice age could've wiped humans out, but we hid in caves to get away from the harsh temperatures. As we move to the future in the ancient Egyptian times, scoliosis existed at this time as well as we evolved from our cave men and women ancestors. King Tutankhamun is now believed to have suffered from Kyphoscoliosis which is a combination of the two kyphosis and scoliosis which curves the thoracic spine backwards (kyphosis) and to be shaped like an S or C (scoliosis). As the results came from a 2010 CAT scan, this made it difficult for him to walk as he was reliant on a walking stick to help his mobility. Many of the disabilities that happened were caused by knowing they had to keep their blood line pure by keeping it in the family and scoliosis was one of the many disabilities that was caused by breeding in the same family.

In Ancient Greece, scoliosis was well documented as Hippocrates (father of modern medicine) founded the condition; he was very interested about learning about it, so he started writing the first description of scoliosis in his medical book. He didn't go into detail in terms of types of scoliosis people had but he knew that he wanted to help them by coming up with treatment methods that would help their symptoms; the popular treatments that he used were called the Hippocrates ladder and the Hippocrates board. Both of these contraptions were designed to pull and stretch the body in an attempt to straighten the spine. The ladder was set up so that the patient would first have their hand tied so they couldn't resist against the treatment and they would be tied to a ladder with their bodies up high and the head either upwards if the curvature was close to the head or upside down if the curvature was lower down possibly in the thoracic region of the spine. This method was using the gravitational force to straighten the spine which had mixed results; some people benefitted while others didn't so. Then he came up with the board where the patient would have their hands and feet tied to both ends of the board, so that somebody could put their hands or feet to add pressure on the spine to help the curved spine or they would use the board to pull the body both upwards and downwards so that the force would attempt to straighten the spine but causing so much pain in the process.

Hippocrates
460 BC-370 BC
Father of Western
Medicine
Founder of Scoliosis

In the second century, another physician took the spotlight into scoliosis; his name was Galen. He was a student at the Hippocratic School of Medicine and agreed with Hippocrates's description of scoliosis and what he did to treat it but at the time, the name scoliosis didn't exist. So, Galen came up with a name we still use today. However, very little improvement was made as many people were still suffering from scoliosis despite the variations of Hippocrates's contraptions. These devices were used until the sixteenth century as there wasn't an alternative treatment method. Soon after the Hippocrates bench was proving to be unpopular. As times changed; new ideas came to shine through.

In the sixteenth century, a new era began for new treatments; an invention that would change the game forever-the brace. You may not think much of it but at this time, it had a vast impact on straightening the spine without causing a massive amount of pain. It was invented by a French surgeon; he was known as the father of modern surgery in his day.

Ambrose was born in Bourg-Hersent which is northwest of France in 1510. As a young child, he was apprenticed by his older brother who was a barber surgeon (who treated solider who went to war). He went with his brother to Hôtel-Dieu which the oldest hospital in France. When Ambrose was 26, he

Ambrose Paré
(1510–20 December 1590)
The founder of the supportive Brace for Scoliosis

joined the French army in 1536 where he spent a lot of time on the battle ground helping the wounded soldiers. He would spend the next 30 years out there inventing new treatments and techniques on helping the injured in particularly war wounds. At this time in battle, surgeons were required to seal the wound with boiling oil. At one point, Ambrose ran out of oil, so he had to make his own cleansing solution with an egg yolk turpentine (tree fluid) and oil of roses and just by a miracle, the solider that he treated was much better than having boiling oil on his wound. Amputation was a common treatment method if they could save a leg or arm from battle, but Ambrose rejected the idea; in fact, he had the idea to use string to tie off the blood vessels. While this was less painful for the patient, it didn't always work as it caused infection and sometimes death, so this idea wasn't taken by other surgeons of this time. This didn't stop him as Ambrose was a thinker and had an interest in inventing new treatment methods for his patients. He designed a corset which was primarily used for children as he thought that the best treatment for adults was to use the Hippocratic bench. The corset provided pressure to the back to give it additional support in the hope that it will soon straighten the spine. The iron corset also featured holes to reduce the weight, so it wouldn't be too heavy for the patient.

Ambrose also realised that if a child had a severe form of scoliosis, then the treatment wouldn't have any affect at all on the spine. Ambrose's brace was notable for being the first of its kind for making an improvement in modern spinal orthotics. In 1552, Ambrose was accepted into the royal service of the Valois Dynasty under King Henry II; however, he was unable to cure King Henry after he suffered from a fatal blow to the head which he received during a jousting tournament in 1559. Ambrose stayed to do his royal duty caring for the royal family until he died in 1590; he also served three other kings, including Francis II, Charles IX and Henry III. At the age of 80, Ambrose died of natural causes on 20 December 1590. Ambrose's brace would be used for another two centuries before someone else had a new idea for treatments.

Lewis Albert Sayre was born in Bottle Hill (Madison) in Morris country, New Jersey. His father was a farmer and the rest of the family was raised to look after the farm. His life changed forever at the age of 10 when his father died and so he moved to live with his uncle who raised him. His uncle was a banker in Lexington Kentucky which allowed him to go to Transylvania University in Lexington in 1839 where he graduated and then moved to the college of physicians and surgeons which is now last of Columbia University. He graduated there in 1843 and was once retained as a surgeon by the college. In 1853, he was appointed surgeon to the Bellevue Hospital and in 1859, surgeon to the Charity Hospital on Blackwell's Island. He became consulting surgeon at the latter institution in 1873. Lewis specialised in injuries and defects in bones and joints in 1861; he was a part of a team of organisers of the Bellevue Hospital Medical College and in the same year, became professor of orthopaedic surgery. He also became professor of clinical surgery and held both chairs until 1898 when the college merged with the New York University and he was made professor of orthopaedic and clinical surgery of the consolidated institution. He was among the founders of the New York Academy of Medicine, the American Medical Association and the New York Pathological Society. He was elected vice president of the American Medical Association in 1866 and its president in 1880; he also helped establish its journal in 1882. Between 1860 and 1866, Sayre acted as health officer for New York City and in that capacity was well respected by the community. In particular, he improved sanitary conditions in New York and secured compulsory vaccinations; he also understood the mechanisms of cholera that were brought by sailors from incoming ships and stopped it from spreading to the city by implementing quarantine. Sayre was renowned for his writings on spinal disorders, especially with regard to the study of scoliosis. During this time, the study of scoliosis was still in its infancy and its origin was widely debated, with the corset being very popular, Sayre criticised it as he believed musculoskeletal imbalance was the primary cause and that treatment should centre on gymnastic exercises to strengthen the muscles on the convex side of

Lewis Albert Sayre
29 February 1820–21
September 1900
Known for his
pioneering
orthopaedic surgery
and for wrapping the
body to correct spinal
deformities.

the deformity. As evidence, he observed that girls who used their corsets infrequently had abnormal spine development. He explained their 'healthy' spines related to their lack of corset use and their being forced to stand erect because of the bundles of wood they constantly carried on their head.

Sayre is best known for his 1874 description of the use of traction in conjunction with a plaster cast to correct and hold spinal deformity. Lewis used a technique similar to what Hippocrates used to correct spinal deformities with the help of traction. Traction was applied by lifting his patient off the ground by supports at the chin and axillae (where the armpits are); following this, a plaster jacket was applied. The plaster jacket, though, was simply used as a treatment method based on the idea of 'gymnastic exercises for cure of the deformity' and consequently was removed at night and during exercise. While Sayre did have some success with his approach, lack of maintenance of correcting eventually led the jacket to be discontinued. His method, however, formed the basis for the next generation of techniques used to treat scoliosis. Throughout his medical career, he faced his fair share of criticism as his pioneering hip joint surgery proved to be technically challenging. In the first few decades after he introduced it. about half of his patients died after the operation and only a few not only recovered but they also gained more flexibility in the hip. Therefore, it was often avoided in favour of non-surgical treatment. In 1849, Lewis married Eliza Ann Hall, a painter from a family of artists; they had three sons and one daughter

Wilhelm Conrad Roentgen 27 March 1845–10 February 1923 (Founder of the X-Ray)

together. All three sons became doctors working with their father, sadly two of the sons died. Charles Henry Hall Sayre from a fall (1850–1880) and Lewis Hall Sayre (1851–1890) from heart disease; his daughter Mary Jane never married and lived with the family, helping her father with his publications. His other son Reginald who was born on 15 October in 1859 became a prominent orthopaedic surgeon and Olympic sport shooter.

The next improvement of scoliosis would involve more scientific methods from a German Physicist Wilhelm Conrad Roentgen. On the evening of 8 November, Wilhelm discovered the X-ray; he did this by using a cathode ray tube in his laboratory which was similar to fluorescent light bulbs which are used today.

He vacuumed all of the oxygen out of the tube and replaced it with a special gas and passed a high electric voltage through it. As the electricity passed through, this produced a fluorescent glow. Wilhelm then shielded the tube with heavy black paper; in doing so, he found that the fluorescent light could be seen even a few feet away from the tube. He realised that he had produced invisible light which was previously unknown. The rays that were being emitted from the tube were capable of travelling through the heavy paper covering the tube. He also found that this new found radiation was capable of travelling through solid objects and they could then be projected onto a piece of film; this was where he named it the X-ray because in mathematics, X was used to be identified as unknown quantity. In his discovery, Wilhelm found that the X-ray would pass the tissue of the human body leaving the bones and the materials visible. One of his first attempts was late in the day of November 1895 was a film of his wife Bertha's hand with a ring on her finger. She was so shocked at the quality of the picture that the only way she could describe it was 'I've just seen my own death' because in those days, you wouldn't see your bones during lifetime. The news of Wilhelm's discovery spread quickly throughout the world. Scientists everywhere could copy his experiment because the cathode tube was very well known at the time.

In early 1896, X-rays were being utilised clinically in America for such things as bone fractures and gunshot wounds. Wilhelm married his wife Anna Bertha Ludwig of Zürich whom he had met in the café run by her father; she was a niece of the poet Otto Ludwig and they married in 1872 in Apeldoorn in the Netherlands. They had no children of their own but they adopted Josephine Bertha Ludwig age six in 1887. She was originally the daughter of Mrs Röntgen's only brother. Four years after his wife, Wilhelm died in Munich on 10 February 1923 from carcinoma (type of cancer) in the intestine.

Legacy

Wilhelm's findings now play a vital role in modern surgery. X-ray and an image of bones inside the body has helped surgeons find the best treatments for people with scoliosis. Physicians before Wilhelm would've had a brief idea of the C and S curvatures of the spine but to actually see it was a real treat for the eyes.

Is Scoliosis Genetic?

Well, as I said before about our ancestors that lived 50,000 years ago, the extreme environment and food played a pivotal role in the DNA as limited food and water was common. The genes therefore suffered and with generation upon generation of not getting enough food, gene mutation was born and copied into other people and spread which caused not only scoliosis but many other disabilities as well. Scoliosis is still passed down from generation to generation; not all cases are biological but the majority of them are. It is unknown where the mutated gene is in our chromosome, but tests are being done. So, overall genetics of scoliosis are complicated to say the least because mutated genes can occur even if it's not in the family tree. So, why does this happen? Well, there's a debate on what caused Scoliosis in the first place-genes or the environment. If you were to ask me which one, I'd say it was a mixture of nutrition and environmental causes which led to our genes to be mutated. With years and years of not getting enough nutrition and tough environments, our genes and cells were going to break down sometime. Tests are being done to find out where the gene is in our chromosome and so in the future, we will be able to tell what the cause is but right now, it's all a mystery.

Scoliosis Today

In terms of treating scoliosis today, nothing much has changed in terms of supporting the spine using braces and casts. In bad cases, surgery to straighten the back is used. We rely on physiotherapy and light exercise to strengthen the spine. Calcium supplants will help strengthen the cartilage as weak cartilage results in the curvature of the spine. In America, it is estimated that scoliosis affects 2–3 per cent of the population which would be around 6–9 million children. In the UK, it is estimated that there are 3–4 per 1,000 people who get scoliosis. The most common are children who are born with it but also as we get older, our calcium levels lowers which gives us more of a chance to get scoliosis as our bones get fragile as we get older. Yet there's no sign of a gene mutation but it could be linked with similar genetics to brittle bones as the cartilage is as weak as brittle bones disease but only in the spine.

Chapter XXII
Parkinson's Disease

Now, if you have come across somebody with Parkinson's (PD), you will know that it's a progressive condition where it affects the nervous system which leads to a defect in motor skills movement and sometimes communication skills. Parkinson's is most common in the elderly but that doesn't mean that Parkinson's can't affect younger people; it's just uncommon to see a young person suffer from PD. There's no cure for Parkinson's but there is medication which helps ease and improve the symptoms.

Symptoms of Parkinson's

The symptoms of Parkinson's are different for everyone. At the beginning, the symptoms may be very mild or even will go unnoticed. Symptoms usually start in one side of the body and they will continue to get worse in that side. Symptoms will progress to the other side of the body as Parkinson's does affect the whole body as it affects the nervous system.

Tremors Tremors or shaking usually begins in arms or legs, often your hand suffers from uncontrollable shaking or fingers. The shaking can last from 5mins to 30mins.

Slowed movement (bradykinesia)-Over time, Parkinson's may slow your movement making simple tasks more difficult and time consuming. Your steps may become shorter when you walk. It may be difficult to get out of a chair. Or you may even drag your feet as you try to walk.

Rigid Muscles Muscle stiffness may occur in any part of the body; the stiff muscles can be painful and limit your range of motion.

Impaired posture and balance Your posture may become stooped, or you may have balance problem as a result of Parkinson's.

Loss of automatic movements You may have decreased ability to perform unconscious movements, including blinking smiling or swinging your arms in the air when you walk.

Speech changes You may speak softly, quickly, slur or hesitate before talking. Your speech may be more of a monotone rather than with usual inflections.

Writing changes It may become harder to write and your writing may appear smaller. As the muscles in your hands get tighter, it can be harder to hold the pen/pencil properly as becomes harder to grip or control it in the paper.

The Causes of Parkinson's Disease

Parkinson's occurs when certain nerve cells or neurones in the brain break down or die. Many of these symptoms are due to the lack of neutrons that produce a chemical messenger in the brain called dopamine. When dopamine levels are low, it causes abnormal brain activity which leads to the symptoms of Parkinson's Disease.

Similar to other disabilities that we've talked about, its causes are governed by two factors-genes and the environment.

Let's start with our genes. There are specific gene mutations that can cause Parkinson's disease. But these are uncommon except in rare cases where many family members are affected by Parkinson's disease. However, certain gene variations appear to increase the chances of Parkinson's disease but with relatively small risk of Parkinson's disease for each of the gene markers.

Environmental Factors

Exposure to certain toxins or environmental causes that affect the nervous system may increase the risk of Parkinson's disease, but the risk is very small.

There Are Other Risk Factors in Regard to:

Age-Parkinson's disease is more common in the elderly. It usually starts either in the middle of your life or late in life. It is mostly common for people to develop the symptoms of Parkinson's in their 60s or over.

Inheritance—If you have close relatives that have Parkinson's, then the chances of getting the condition is increased; however, the chances of getting the disease is smaller if you only have 1 or 2 members of the family that have it.

Gender-Men are more likely to get Parkinson's than women according to a test that was published in 2000 by the American Academy of Neurology. The test was conducted by following a group of 4,341 elderly people; none of them showed any signs of the symptoms; however, during the time of the test, 29 men and 13 women later on developed the symptoms of Parkinson's, a further 14 men and 12 women developed the disease which was due to other causes such as dementia or a stroke.

The Rate of Getting Parkinson's Disease

In the United States, about one million Americans are thought to have Parkinson's which is more than people who have Multiple Sclerosis (MS), Muscular Dystrophy (MD), Amyotrophic Lateral Sclerosis (ALS) combined. Every year, about 60,000 Americans are diagnosed with Parkinson's. These results can easily change as many more Americans suffer with the disease without a diagnosis.

In Canada, roughly 100,000 Canadians are living with Parkinson's disease, with roughly 6,600 people being diagnosed every year.

In the United Kingdom, it's a little bit more than Canada with roughly 127,000 people. In the UK, someone is diagnosed with Parkinson's every hour and most of them are 50 or over.

The History of Parkinson's

We come to the main question, where did it all begin for Parkinson's? As a matter of fact, in the beginning it wasn't called Parkinson's at all; it was called shaking palsy by a man called James Parkinson as he published his essay on the disease. In the first chapter of his essay, he briefly describes Parkinson's with 'involuntary tremulous motion with lessened muscular power in parts not in action even when supported; with a propensity to bend the trunk forwards and to pass from a walking pace to a running pace. The senses and the intellect are left uninjured'. So, even in this brief text, he talks about how the muscles in the limbs uncontrollably shake which leads the body to be paralysed by it. Towards the end of the passage, he writes about the progressive nature of Parkinson's which is how we know it today. Surprisingly though, even before James Parkinson wrote his essay is that James wasn't the first person to write about Parkinson's. Evidence suggests that Parkinson's was first described by the ancient Egyptians in the Ebers Papyrus (world's oldest medical document) in the 12th century BC; it explains how an Egyptian King was left drooling with uncontrollable arms from aging. Galen wrote about Parkinson's as well; he describes it as a disease that you get when you are close to rest; the body is left paralysed with postural changes. Galen's references still resonated with people until the seventeenth century. More descriptions on Parkinson's kept flooding in, from other physicians such as Johannes Baptiste Sager and Hieronymus David Gaubius where they described Parkinson's as festination (Parkinson's Gait) which is a characteristic trait which explains how the motor skills in the muscles slow down during the course of having Parkinson's. John Hunter a Scottish surgeon who was around just before James Parkinson, provided a really thorough description of Parkinson's disease but this time, he described it as paralysis agitans which is an older term for Parkinson's and is also used to describe the loss of motor and sensory skills. Finally, Auguste François Chomel like James provided an essay on Parkinson's which included several descriptions of abnormal muscle movements.

In 1817, James Parkinson became famous when he published his essay reporting six cases of what he called paralysis agitans. An Essay on the Shaking Palsy described a characteristic trait for resting tremors, abnormal posture and gait (difficulty in walking), paralysis and weakening muscle strength, and the way that the disease progresses over time. He also acknowledged and paid tribute to the contributions of many of the previously mentioned authors, surgeons and physicians of their vital research and understanding of PD. Although the article, was later considered as a pioneering the work on the disease, received little attention over the forty years that followed. Furthermore, the term paralysis agitans was at this time applied to any condition with a loss of motor activity accompanied by seizures. Indeed, the term 'paralysis' alone included both motor and sensory disorders. Another important figure in PD was William Sanders. He proposed in 1865 that the term Parkinson's Disease be used for the onset of symptoms in older people; it had been described as paralysis agitans festation of the sensors of Parkinson's disease.

Neurologists who made further additions to the knowledge of the disease include Trousseau, Gowers, Kinnier Wilson and Erb, and most notably Charcot, whose studies between 1868 and 1881 were a landmark in the understanding of the disease. Among other advances, he made the distinction between rigidity, weakness and bradykinesia (slowness of movement). He also championed the idea of renaming the disease after James Parkinson's Disease in honour of his work and dedication to PD.

Twentieth Century

As a new century arose, physicians wanted to find out where PD actually started from. The first speculations of PD were made 80 years after Parkinson's essay, when Édouard Brissaud proposed an idea that it had its origin in the subthalamus or cerebral peduncle and might be caused by an ischemic lesion (Restricted blood flow). In 1912, Frederic Lewy described a pathologic finding in affected brains, later named 'Lewy bodies'. Frederic found abnormal protein activity in the brain which caused people to act differently. However, scientists at this time couldn't prove this, so in 1919, Konstantin Tretiakoff reported that the substantia nigra (located in the mid brain which is for movement and reward) was the main cerebral structure affected, but this finding was not accepted until it was confirmed by further studies published by Rolf Hassler in 1938. He underlined the biochemical changes in the brain but again wasn't confirmed until the 1950s, due to the work of Arvid Carlsson on the neurotransmitter dopamine and Oleh Hornykiewicz on its role on PD. Carlsson was eventually awarded a Nobel Prize for this work.

Alice Lazzarini pinpointed a genetic component to PD in 1994. Years earlier, the neurology clinic at Robert Wood Johnson Medical School (RWJMS) had located a family of Italian origin that encompassed at least five generations of more than 400 individuals and at least 60 members with PD, and traced their ancestors to the small village of Contursi, Italy.

The Discovery of the Gene Mutation

In 1995, the RWJMS team joined with the National Centre for Human Genome Research at the National Institutes of Health took advantage of the laboratory resources available from the NIH in an effort to locate the gene causing PD in the Contursi family. The team reported the first Parkinson disease-causing mutation. They named the gene mutation PARK1 in the brain protein, alpha-synuclein (The main protein structure in the brain and the heart). Within days of the publication of the PARK1 findings, alpha-synuclein was discovered to be the major component of Lewy bodies which also answered Frederic's unanswered theory. Within brain cells of PD patients, the location of the PARK 1 gene is quite easy to spot as it's quite large compared to the other mutated genes. It is located in chromosome 4 at position 22.1. This discovery changed the direction of research into PD by providing scientists with an entirely new protein whose manufacture, function or breakdown could be the key to the disease. Synuclein proteins being the main component of Lewy bodies was discovered in 1997 by Spillantini, Trojanowski, Goedert and others. Towards the late 90s and the beginning of the 2000s, new gene mutations in the PARK 1 gene were found; autosomal recessive juvenile Parkinsonism were discovered in 1998.

Finally, between 2002–2005, PARK 1 gene mutations and the most common mutations in the LKKR2 gene were identified in Japanese and European families. The diagnostic staging of Parkinson's disease was described by Heiko Braak in 2003, saying how Parkinson's starts in older people.

The Treatment of Parkinson's Disease

There are many treatments that are considered for Parkinson's. There is medication to help slow down the symptoms of Parkinson's but not necessarily cure it. Some people use acupuncture or therapy to try and relieve the stress factors that may cause the symptoms to get worse or they can choose to take medicine to treat Parkinson's; there are seven different medications that are currently treating it which is primarily made to increase or stop the levels of dopamine from being too low which causes the symptoms.

Carbidopa-Levodopa

This medication is mostly known as Levodopa which is the most effective medication for Parkinson's. It is a natural chemical that passes into the brain; as it gets to the brain, the brain converts it into dopamine which is what patients need. The Carbidopa (Lodosyn) plays a role in protecting the Levodopa from early conversion to dopamine; this prevents or lessens the effects of the medication such as nausea, light-headedness. However, there is a drawback to this medicine. After a patient who has been taking it for years, the effects can wear off leading the progressive nature of Parkinson's to takeover.

Carbidopa-Levodopa Infusion

This medication is the same as the first; just that it is put into the body differently by using feeding tubes, the medication is in a gel form so it is easier for it travel down into the small intestine. This way of treating Parkinson's is for patients with severe cases of the condition. A feeding tube is needed if a patient can't swallow or can't take in medication for other reasons. Surgery is needed to place the feeding tubes inside the body which is inserted through the skin close to the stomach, then puncturing a tiny hole into the stomach so that a tiny wire can go inside the stomach. In order for the brain to convert the Levodopa into dopamine, it needs to go through the small intestines which is done by passing the wire through the small intestine, so that the gel liquid can pass the stomach and the small intestine. This procedure does have its risks; most common is infection but as long as it's clean, the risks are very low.

Dopamine Agonists

Dopamine Agonists is different from the Levodopa medication; instead of changing into dopamine as Levodopa does it mimics the effects in the brain. Basing in mind they aren't as effective as Levodopa. But they last longer and maybe used with Levodopa to smooth the on and off effects of Levodopa. Some of the side effects are similar to Levodopa but they can also cause the patient to hallucinate, drowsiness, this medication can also cause compulsive behaviour changes such as increase in sex drive, gambling and eating. If you have any concerns on thieve side effects, I recommend you see a doctor.

MAO B Inhibitors

These medications help prevent the breakdown of dopamine in the brain, by inhibiting the brain's enzyme monoamine oxidase. This enzyme metabolises brain dopamine; side effects may include nausea or insomnia. If your doctor prescribes you this medication with levodopa, this may cause hallucinations as well.

Catechol O-Methyltransferase (COMT) Inhibitors

This medication mildly prolongs the effects of Levodopa therapy by blocking an enzyme that breaks down dopamine. Side effects include increased risk of involuntary movements (dyskinesia) mainly from enhanced Levodopa effects. Other side effects include diarrhoea or other side effects.

Anticholinergics

This medication is an older medication that was used for many years to help control tremors associated with Parkinson's Disease. Several medications are still available which include benztropine (cogentin) or trihexyphenidyl.

However, these medications are rarely prescribed by doctors in recent times as they are known to cause bad side effects such as impaired memory, confusion hallucinations, dry mouth and weak bladder.

Amantadine

Doctors may prescribe Amantadine to provide short-term relief of symptoms with patients showing mild signs of Parkinson's disease. To control involuntary movements (dyskinesia) which are induced by Carbidopa Levodopa. Side effects may include your skin to change colour (purple), ankle swelling or hallucinations.

Deep Brain Stimulation (DBS)

There's one surgery that surgeons used to treat Parkinson's-Deep Brian Stimulation which involves the surgeon to drill a tiny whole through the top of the head and insert tiny electrodes through the brain and into the lower centre of the brain (close to the top of the spinal cord); the electrodes are attached to a generator which is also implanted inside the chest near the collarbone which sends electronic pulses to your brain which is meant to reduce the symptoms of Parkinson's Disease. Your doctor may be required to change the settings when necessary to treat your condition. Like with all surgeries, it has its risks which include infection, stroke or brain haemorrhage. Some people experience problems with DBS system or have complications due to stimulation and your doctor may need to adjust or replace some parts of the system. DBS is most often offered to people with really advanced Parkinson's who have unstable medication (Levodopa) responses. DBS can stabilise medication fluctuations, reduce or halt involuntary movements (dyskinesia), reduce tremor, reduce weakness in the muscles and improve slowing of movement. DBS is effective in controlling erratic and fluctuating responses to Levodopa or controlling dyskinesia that doesn't improve with medication alone. However, DBS isn't helpful for a problem that doesn't respond to Levodopa therapy apart from tremor. A tremor may be controlled by DBS even if the tremor isn't very responsive to Levodopa. DBS may provide hope for people with Parkinson's Disease if it helps the disease from progressing.

Parkinson's Disease and Its Related Illnesses

There are currently seven different types of Parkinson's which are most common throughout Europe, but it can happen worldwide these are:

Corticobasal Degeneration

Corticobasal Parkinson's is a rare type which usually affects 40–50 even 70-year-old people. It usually affects one side of the body and then it can slowly progress to affecting both sides. It has similarities to Progressive Supranuclear Palsy; in some cases, patients even go on to develop Progressive Supranuclear Palsy and Corticobasal Degeneration could develop if they started having Progressive Supranuclear Palsy. Symptoms include:

Difficulty in controlling limbs.

Numbness or loss of coordination.

Muscle stiffness.

Shaking (tremor).

Jerky movements or muscle spasms.

Balance and coordination problems.

Swallowing difficulties.

Memory problems.

Corticobasal Degeneration is caused when brain cells in the cortex and basil ganglia regions of the brain are damaged; this occurs when a protein called TAU builds up over time causing massive clumps which are responsible for nerve damage. In a healthy brain, the protein breaks down to avoid the build-up which damages the nerves. There are rumours that it is passed down from your parents through genes. The chances of that happening are very low.

To treat it, medication can help regain movement in the limbs and gain some function but medication alone isn't enough to treat it, so therapy is recommended; such as physiotherapy to gain motor functions in our arms and legs and help to regain balance. Speech and language therapy are needed to regain communication skills and help with swallowing. An occupational therapist can help arrange different equipment and helping adapt the patient's lifestyle in the home. They can also help by coming up with strategic methods to help with daily tasks, both at home and life in general, more importantly to gain independence.

Dementia with Lewy Bodies

This type is a form of dementia, but it also has a progressive nature in destroying the body. The patient will have good and bad days. They may see things that aren't really there (Hallucinate), their muscles may get stiffer as well as uncontrollable shaking can be experienced. Lewy Bodies Dementia is less common than Alzheimer's and Dementia. It's only responsible for 20% of all dementia cases worldwide. No one truly knows the causes of Lewy bodies but nerve cells and neurone in the brain die; this can be from ageing, damage to the brain in any form. Genetics don't yet provide a certain answer either, if more family members have this condition, the chances of passing it into your children are still very low.

Drug Induced Parkinson's

This is very rare to develop. Parkinson's can be a result of certain drugs that someone takes. This happens when the medication blocks the actions of dopamine. Dopamine plays a role in maintaining muscle movement. The main drugs that are responsible for decreasing dopamine levels are neuroleptic or antipsychotic drugs used to treat schizophrenia and other psychiatric problems.

Prochlorperazine (Stemetil) used to treat dizziness and nausea.

Metoclopromide (Maxolon, Plasil) used to treat nausea and indigestion.

It is incredibly rare for symptoms to get worse through other drugs. If the patient is guided to stop taking the medication, if they can and move onto drugs which helps dopamine levels, then symptoms of Parkinson's should improve as well.

Tremor

With tremors, it is the cause of uncontrollable shaking which starts affecting the hands and arms and slowly progresses to the legs, head and even speech. There's not yet a known cause; however, we do know that there's a 50% chance of getting it from your parents through genes. If not, it becomes more likely with age; the brain cells start to die out which causes the tremors on patient's face. Tremors often gets confused with Parkinson's as both have uncontrollable shaking but with tremors, the shaking isn't as violent as with Parkinson's.

Multiple System Atrophy

This type is a neurological disorder which is a progressive deterioration of the nervous system. This is caused by an over production of a protein called alpha synuclein which causes the degeneration of nerve cells (Atrophy). Both men and women can be affected by (MSA); it affects mostly 30–60-year-olds, although it can affect people that are older but that's where it starts. MSA is not contagious nor infectious.

The Symptoms of MSA:

- slowed movements,
- rigidity or stiffness,
- difficulty turning in bed,
- difficulty in initiating a movement,
- difficulty writing; writing may become small and spidery,
- loss of balance and poor coordination or clumsiness (ataxia),
- speech difficulties,
- difficulty with fine motor skills such as doing up buttons,
- problems with erection or male impotence,
- loss of bladder control, including urgency, frequent urination or incomplete emptying, often getting up several times at night to pass urine,
- bowel problems, including constipation,
- inability to sweat,
- cold hands and feet,
- drop in blood pressure when standing (postural hypotension), leading to dizziness, fainting or blurred vision,
- coat hanger pain (pain in neck or shoulders) as a result of low blood pressure,
- problems with swallowing,
- emotions that are easily aroused or tend to change quickly,
- depression, anxiety or a feeling of being overwhelmed,
- soft voice, particularly when tired,
- restless sleep,
- noisy breathing, including snoring when sleeping.

Progressive Supranuclear Palsy (PSP)

Progressive Supranuclear Palsy is an unknown type of Parkinson's. It is often confused with being the same as Parkinson's as they have similar symptoms, being that the neurones slowly die out which results in loss of muscle function and uncontrollable shaking which is what Parkinson's is known for. The difference is that PSP in the early stages progresses a lot faster than Parkinson's. PSP also doesn't respond as well to Parkinson's medication as the symptoms are worse.

The symptoms include:

- poor balance and unsteady gait or walking,
- frequent falls, generally backwards,
- slowed movements,
- rigidity or stiffness,
- cramped writing,
- blurred eyesight, gaze palsy (the inability to look up or down), slow blinking, difficulty in maintaining eye contact, tunnel vision and sensitivity to light,
- soft, slow, and slurred speech,
- difficulty in swallowing,
- anxiety and/or depression, and loss of motivation,
- forgetfulness,
- personality change (loss of interest in ordinary pleasurable activities or increased irritability; difficulty resisting impulses; inappropriate behaviour),
- difficulty synthesising several different ideas into a new idea or plan,
- slowing of thought difficulty finding words (aphasia).

In terms of treating PSP, it's very complex condition which will need more than one approach to treat it. However, around 20–30% of patients who have PSP respond pretty well to the medication Levodopa

Vascular Arteriosclerosis Parkinson's (VAP)

VAP affects people when they have a low blood supply to the brain which leads to a stroke. Patients who have suffered a stroke later on develop symptoms similar to Parkinson's which makes so hard to tell the differences between the two. The most common symptoms they'll experience are uncontrollable shaking, memory problems and sleeping which can affect your mood.

These types are mostly picked up from other illnesses which leads to Parkinson's and helps doctors diagnose patients with what type of Parkinson's they have, which makes it easier to treat the Parkinson's that they have.

The man who discovered Parkinson's Disease.

James Parkinson 11 April 1755–21 December 1824 Who Discovered Parkinson's Disease

James Parkinson was born in Shropshire in London, England in 1755. His parents were called Mary and John Parkinson. James was the oldest and the followed by his younger sister Mary and his younger Brother William. His father was a doctor which had a big influence on James, so in 1776, aged 21, he decided to go to the London Hospital where he took being a doctor very seriously and in 1800, James received a medical leaflet known as the hospital pupil; he read it to understand the system of how medical education was applied to people. James's interest in medicine really took hold and he became really knowledgeable by this time. Sadly, he suffered a personal blow; after the death of his father, John was more determined to make it in medicine. By doing so, he received a diploma in the Royal College of Surgeons. He later worked as a general practitioner in Hoxton (Shoreditch) for over a decade. James was elected president of the medical society of London in 1817. He also published his essay called the shaking palsy. In that, he described the six symptoms of Parkinson's disease-involuntary tremors, weakened muscle power, bending over whilst trying to walk (Parkinson's gait); his landmark discoveries made 140 before levodopa was used to treat Parkinson's. The founder of modern neurology Jean-Martin Charcot renamed the condition 60 years later.

While James was popular in medicine, he also had other passions in politics. He was very strong advocate for the underprivileged and also wasn't shy to voice his opinion on the government of his day. Even early in his career, he fought for social and revolutionary causes. James got into controversy at times because he was an advocate for the French Revolution; a lot of people at this time didn't like it despite Britain being in a political crisis itself. James had published 20 leaflets after the French Revolution calling for social reform and universal suffrage so that everyone could vote. Parkinson later called for representation of the people in the House of Commons; he was then later to become a member of secret political societies, including the London Corresponding Society and the society for constitutional information. In 1794, his membership was to be examined under oath before William Pitt (prime minister) and the privy council. him, but his close friends were sent to prison for many months before being free. On 21 May 1783, James married his wife Mary Dale and they had eight children, two of which died in infancy. After he was married, he succeeded his father's practice and went on to spend the most of his medical career at 1 Hoxton Square.

On 21 December, James sadly died after suffering from a stroke which caused him to lose the ability to talk. He left his houses in Langthorne to his sons and his wife. Most of his belongings were left for his wife. He was left buried at St Leonard's Church in Shoreditch.

Legacy

James's legacy is one of the greatest journeys we've been on; to have a condition named after you must be the most incredible feeling and to fight for the people with his activism, I think makes him one of the greats.

Parkinson's Disease Today

Parkinson's has certainly come a long way because at the start of its history, it was a little-known illness, with very little ideas to treat it. Over time, science and medicine have become more advanced and created so many treatments over the years in terms of medications and even surgeries to help manage the symptoms of Parkinson's. People with Parkinson's are reliant on support from doctors to help them through the tough times.

Chapter XXIII
Down Syndrome

Lastly, by no means least, we come to our final disability; thank you for making it this far on our journey. We come to Down syndrome. Down Syndrome or (DS or DNS) also known as trisomy 21 is a genetic disorder where chromosome 21 (hence the name trisomy 21) has a third copy either partially or completely as the genes grow when the baby is in the womb. This is because either a sperm cell or an egg cell has an extra copy of chromosome 21 before or during conception. It is usually related to physical growth delays. The person will grow up to have intellectual disabilities and characteristic facial features. The average IQ of a young adult with DS is 50 which is the equivalent to the mental capacity of an— or 9-year-old child but this can vary widely. As I believe that you can teach a child with Down Syndrome anything you'd like, but you need patience, commitment and love along the way. The parents of children with DS usually have genetically normal genes but the probability increases, studies show, when the parent is older. 0.1% chance of your baby getting Down syndrome if you are 20 years old or less but if you leave it until 40–45 years or more, then it's an increase of 3% for the extra chromosome to arise. It may also explain the statistic that women who are 30 or younger have the chance of 1 in 1000 of having a child with Down Syndrome. For women who are older than 45, the birth rate goes up to 12 in 1,000 babies born to have Down Syndrome.

Characteristics of Down Syndrome

Eyes that slant upwards, skin folds on the inner corner of the eye, they can have white spots on the iris.

Children will experience low muscle tone.

Small stature and a short neck.

A flat nasal bridge.

Single deep creases across the centre of the palms.

A protruding tongue (sticks out).

A large space between the big toe and the second toe.

A bend of the fifth finger which is caused by a growth defect called clinodactyly.

Life for children with Down Syndrome certainly doesn't go without its challenges as they have cognitive development that means that they have mild to moderate intellectual disabilities. Like I said, any child with DS with the right support, patience and love can achieve great things; they will just do things differently than others. Children with Down Syndrome often reach development milestones a little later than other children. For example, in learning how to speak, they may need to have speech therapy in order to achieve the right pronunciation. Motor skills maybe delayed; they may take longer in learning how to walk and grabbing things with their hands. On an average, children will learn how to sit at 11 months, to crawl at 17 months and to walk when they are 26 months old. They may also have difficulties in concentrating on tasks, a tendency to make poor judgements and impulsive behaviour. However, most people with DS can attend school and become active and valued members of society. There are other health issues that comes with Down Syndrome as well; around half of people with DS have congenital heart defects. Other problems may include:

Respiratory problems.

Hearing difficulties.

Alzheimer's Disease.

Leukaemia.

Epilepsy.

Thyroid conditions.

Despite this, there seems to be lower risks of hardening of the arteries, diabetic retinopathy and most kinds of cancer.

Mosaic Down syndrome

This type of Down Syndrome that is not well known is mosaic down syndrome this is diagnosed when there is a mixture of cells that lies in our chromosomes; some chromosomes have the usual 46 cells in our chromosomes some have 47; the chromosome with 47 cells gets copied for the third time. This is a more uncommon type of DS than the main type known as Trisomy 21. There's only 1% chance of getting (MDS) for all down syndrome cases. Research shows that people with MDS have less characteristics than the main type of DS.

Translocation

This is where it can be quite confusing as this type of down syndrome like the previous two has three chromosome 21s; however, translocation comes in when the third copy of the chromosome moves away and attaches to another chromosome; most commonly, it attaches to chromosome 14 which still presents the characteristics of DS; the only difference is that the chromosome move to another one. This isn't as rare as MSD but it's still rare as it affects only 4% of all cases of down syndrome.

Who Discovered Down Syndrome?

John Langdon Down
18 November 1828–7
October 1896
Founder of Down
Syndrome

The man who discovered DS was a British physician called John Langdon Down who was born in Torpoint in Cornwall on 18 November 1828; he was the son of a village grocer and was the sixth child of a very religious family. He helped his family work the family business until he was 18. Besides working in the family business, he also had a fascination in working as a pharmacist, so in his free time, he would read medical books to take in as much information as he could. Shortly after, he qualified as a pharmacist before entering medical school at the London Hospital. He won numerous medals and prizes and immediately after taking his medical degree, he was appointed medical superintendent of Royal Earlswood Asylum for mentally ill in Surrey. Bearing in mind he had no medical knowledge in how to help the people of Earlswood, he reformed the institution and his efforts at classification resulted in his description of what he called Mongolian idiocy which was the first name of DS. His findings were based on measurements—diameters of the head and of the palate to measure intelligence; the larger the head, the more intelligent you were. John also came across a book written by Johan Friedrich Blumenbach a German Physician in which he explained different types of social groups that would lead us to have different abilities of learning and how different people's intellect was based on these groups. In his book, he had five different groups which were defined by head measurements:

Caucasian

Mongolian

Ethiopian

American

Malayans (people from Malaysia)

Blumenbach believed that certain characteristics for the body to look different from others were due to different environments and dietary conditions. Blumenbach's comparative anatomy was really popular at the time, so much so that it was translated into English by Bendyshe Laydon. John read the book and the knowledge interested him. John took his new found information and named the people of Earlswood Asylum one of Johan's social groups upon the evidence of measuring their heads and the identification of the facial features that John found and he took over 200 pictures of people with Down Syndrome. There were sadly some downsides as John had the idea of calling them after the Mongolian social group; the public wasn't keen on this idea at all; in fact, he was really criticised by the public and was sometimes called a racist. But he stuck by his opinions by saying that the Mongolian group had some similarities as they had the facial features as we associate with DS today.

John wasn't being rude; it was just that it was very common at this time that terms idiots and Mongols were used to describe the disabled but the public were beginning to see that this type of language wasn't acceptable to describe disabled people. In his defence, he wrote a second medical paper in stating that 'a very large number of congenital outcasts are typical Mongols, I shall describe an idiot member of this racial division selected from the large number that have fallen under my observation'. He goes on to describe what a Mongol looked like-'the hair is not black as in the real Mongol but brownish colour, straight and scanty. The face is flat and broad and destitute of prominence. The checks are roundish and extended sideways. The eyes are roundish and the internalise more than normally distant from one another. The Eyelids open very narrow. The forehead is wrinkled the lips are large and thick with transverse openings. The tongue is long thick and rough. The nose is small the skin has slight dirty yellowish tinge, and is deficient in elasticity, giving the appearance of being too large for the body'. Shortly after publishing this description to the hospital in London, things started to change as the condition mongolism was changed to be named after him as Down Syndrome as we know it today. Sadly, John wasn't alive as it wasn't until the 1970s where people began to realise his impact associated with Down Syndrome.

Personal Life

In the 1850s, John went back to Torpoint to visit his sister Sarah but shortly after, he met a woman who would later become his future wife Mary Crellin. They both fell in love with each other but they knew that they couldn't marry or start a family because John wasn't earning any money. It was when John started working at Earlswood, that they started to save their money and got married 10 October 1860. Both Mary and John had a lot in common; both of them had fathers who were strong businessmen, and both were religious which was really important to the both of them and eventually John's career went from strength to strength and had four children along the way. Their first son was called Everleigh Langdon Down; he was born a year after they got married. Everleigh began work as a solider but at the age of 22, he had seriously injured himself with a chisel. His injuries were so bad that the doctors tried their best to heal his wounds, but it wasn't enough; he sadly died as a result. Their second child was a daughter called Lillian Langdon Down; she was the only daughter that they had. She was also born in Earlswood; she was seriously ill throughout her short life and only lived for two years. Doctors thought that she may have had a virus in her brain and she was seriously ill in the last two weeks of her life and sadly died on 1 June 1865. The third child was Reginald Langdon Down; he was born in Earlswood on 4 August 1866 and lastly, they had another son called Percival Langdon Down who was born on the 6 May 1868. Both sons had a good education and went to school and university; they both studied medicine just like his father. Later on, they both continued the work that their father had started working in both Normansfield and London where John had his practice. In the winter of 1890, John suffered from a severe flu; he recovered from it slowly but his body was slowly shutting down as his heart was having problems for which he took pills He couldn't work as he was deteriorating but he still turned up to watch and advise his sons. Six years later on the 7 October 1896, he died which happened very suddenly. The family were sad to see him go, especially his wife Mary. In her husband's memory, Mary kept on working in Normansfield. In the year 1900, there was a flu epidemic and Mary was deeply affected. She died from it and was buried next to her husband John.

Legacy

Remembering John I think is really important because unlike the rest of the people that grew up in medicine or had family in medicine, John didn't have that; he went with his gut to try medicine for himself and he had to learn the trade as he went, even though he had no knowledge of helping people with disabilities, he was always intrigued and willing to help them.

Professor Jérôme Lejeune (13 June 1926–3 April 1994) (Founder of Trisomy 21) (Father of modern Genetics)

There is one more person that played a huge role in the history of Down Syndrome, one that found an important piece of a big puzzle. This was Professor **Jerome Lejeune.**

Professor Jérôme was born on 13 June 1926 in Montrouge, France. From a very early age, he wanted to become a doctor; not only was he interested in medicine, but he also liked mathematics, astronomy, music and the theatre. After WWII had ended, he decided to choose his life path in medicine. In 1951, he became an assistant to Professor Turpin; he was concerned for patients who were known as Mongols at the time. He decided to dedicate his life to helping people with Down Syndrome and finding a cure would become his life mission.

In 1958, Jérôme looked into the chromosomes of a young boy who had Down Syndrome. What he found was something different happened with chromosome 21 there weren't two of them. Lehigh would happen to a normal person; the chromosome had copied three times. At the time, this must've been utterly mind blowing to see at first; other doctors didn't believe Jérôme; they thought he made it up. But he knew what he found was right, so he published his first medical paper with the help of Professor Turpin which had three Mongol children who had the third copy of chromosome 21. Shortly after his medical paper was published, the international community of medicine slowly started to realise the significance of his discovery. From then, Jérôme's life had changed; he began to receive awards, he received memberships to international academies and institutions. In his later work, he found another condition which like Down Syndrome related to gene mutations. In 1963, he found that chromosome 5 had a missing part at the end of the chromosome which resulted in causing Cri du Chat Syndrome.

Symptoms of Cri Du Syndrome include:

- High pitch voice.
- Weak muscle tone.
- Children tend to learn slower than other children in school.
- Distinctive facial features.
- Difficulty in learning language so they learn it though other ways by learning gestures or sign language.
- Small head.
- Wide spaced eyes.
- More likely to turn deaf.

Other characteristics may include feeding difficulties, delays in walking, hyperactive, scoliosis, organ failure (rare occasion) but on the whole, people with Cri Du Chat Syndrome have normal life expectancies.

Treating Cri Du Chat Syndrome: Sadly, there isn't any specific treatment that works at the moment but children who have the right support from medical teams, parents and therapists can achieve their highest potential with early and constant educational help as well as physical and language therapy.

In 1966, he described 18Q Syndrome which included:

- Short stature.
- Difficulty in learning new skills.
- Weak muscles.
- Abnormal growth in the hands and feet.
- Abnormalities of the face and skull such as small head.
- Prominent ears, carp shape mouth, deeply set eyes.
- Vision and hearing impairments.
- Heart defects.
- Epilepsy.
- Display signs of autism.

It's estimated that 1 in 55,000 children worldwide are born with 18Q syndrome which makes this a very rare disease. He later on discovered two more gene mutations in chromosomes 8 and 9; like in the case of Down Syndrome chromosomes 8 and 9 had a third copy.

Chromosome 8 Trisomy Symptoms:

Distinctive facial features, elongation of the skull (scaphocephaly,) wide spaced eyes, deeply set eyes, broad upturned nose and a smaller mouth than normal which can cause dental problems because there isn't enough room to fit the teeth. There's nothing much doctors can do except making sure that there is enough air flow for the patient to breathe.

Brain malformations.

Highly arched or cleft palate.

Shortened neck with skin folds.

Long slim body with narrow hip, shoulders and pelvis.

Kidney and cardiac abnormalities.

Permanently bent fingers and stiff joints.

Abnormally malformed kneecaps.

Scoliosis.

Eye abnormalities.

Most people with Trisomy 8 have a moderate amount of intelligence ranging from 50 to 75 with an IQ test and some have a normal range of intelligence. So far, there is no connection on how Trisomy 8 affects intelligence. But there seems to be an increased risk of infections and certain cancers as Wilms tumour, (kidney cancer), acute myeloid leukaemia and myelodysplasia which is a group of illnesses which is caused by poorly formed red blood cells or red blood cells that don't work properly. This is a list of the symptoms:

- Fatigue.
- Shortness of breath.
- Unusual paleness which occurs due to a low red blood cell count (anaemia).
- Easy or unusual bruising or bleeding which occurs due to a low blood platelet count (thrombocytopenia).
- Pinpoint-sized red spots just beneath your skin caused by bleeding (petechiae).
- Frequent infections which occurs due to a low white blood cell count (leukopenia).
- Treatments for myelodysplasia.
- Blood transfusions.

- Blood transfusions can be used to replace red blood cells, white blood cells or platelets in people with myelodysplastic syndromes.
- Medications.
- Now different medication comes in different categories for the different symptoms that myelodysplasia has.
- Increase the number of blood cells your body makes.
- these medications are artificial versions of substances found naturally in your bone marrow as bone marrow is responsible for maturing the vital red blood cells needed to fight infection.

Stimulate Blood Cells to Mature

Medications such as azacitidine (Vidaza) and decitabine (Dacogen) might improve the quality of life of people with certain myelodysplastic syndromes and reduce the risk of acute myelogenous leukaemia.

Suppress Your Immune System

These types of medications are used in certain myelodysplastic syndromes and might lessen the need for red blood cell transfusions.

These help people with a certain genetic abnormality.

If your myelodysplastic symptoms are associated with a gene mutation called isolated del(5q), your doctor might recommend lenalidomide (Revlimid).

Treat Infections

If your condition causes you to have infections, you'll be treated with antibiotics.

We Come to Chromosome 9 Trisomy

This is when a baby is born with a third copy of the chromosome 9; it's incredibly rare. Trisomy conditions like this one aren't inherited; it's just that the genes mutate on their own.

Symptoms

Small head, sloping forehead, broad nose with a bulging tip, slit like nostrils, small jaw, cleft lip or palate, low set misshapen ears; microphthalmia, small eyes and slanting eye lid folds, delays in development and intellectual learning, abnormal growth, low birth weight, low muscle tone and short stature.

Vision Problems

Congenital heart defects

Abnormalities of the muscles and bones as congenital dislocation of the hips, abnormal position or limited function of the joints, underdevelopment of certain bones and abnormal curvature of the spine.

Unusually formed feet such as club foot or flat feet.

Abnormalities of the male reproductive system including undescended testicles, small penis, or abnormal placement of the urinary opening.

Kidney Problems

Brain malformations such as hydrocephalus and dandy walker malformation.

Treatment

Similar to chromosome 8 Trisomy, chromosome 9 Trisomy is dealt with a medical management team that provides medical support for the patient with physicians, therapists, doctors, teachers, and parents can provide care love and support for these children that come into the world then there is no reason why they can't live a normal happy life.

He discovered the trisomy in chromosomes 8 & 9 in 1970 and 1971. But in 1962, the president of the United States presented him with the Kennedy Prize. In 1963, before the French presentation of medicine, he explained how the absence of a specific segment in the genome could result in a disease. In 1964, the first chair of human genetics was created at the Paris School of Medicine, and Lejeune was named to fill it. The appointment was highly unusual: only a ground-breaking discovery allowed a candidate to be named a professor of medicine without successfully completing a competitive residency examination. In 1969, Lejeune's work earned him the William Allan Award, granted by the American Society of Human Genetics, the world's highest honour in genetics. Since then, he's the only French man to receive this award.

Pro Life Work

Jérôme did a lot of work promoting Pro-life work.

Although Jérôme's discoveries paved the way for new research into how changes in gene copy number could cause disease, they also led to the development of prenatal diagnosis of chromosome abnormalities and to abortions of affected pregnancies. This was very distressing to him as he was a devoted Catholic and led him to begin his fight for the pro-life cause.

In 1967, Jérôme opposed the authorisation for women to use contraception as well as the Peyret Laws in 1970 to render legal the interruption of pregnancy in case of foetal abnormalities. He also opposed the Veil Law 1974 (which allowed women to have an abortion if the woman wanted one without being prosecuted by the French government).

After receiving the Allan Prize, Lejeune gave a talk to his colleagues which concluded by explicitly questioning the morality of abortion, an unpopular viewpoint in the profession. The majority of his colleagues disagreed with Jérôme which felt like a defeat for him as they still were with Veil Law as it stood to protect women who wanted an abortion. In a letter to his wife, Lejeune wrote, "Today, I lost my Nobel prize in Medicine." It didn't stop him from continuing his talks about prolife as he continued.

In 1975, after one of his public appearances in Paris, Lejeune met Wanda Poltawska, director of the Catholic Institute for the Family in Krakow in southern Poland. Later that year, Wanda contacted Jérôme twice, asking him to speak at conferences on the beginning of life that she was organising with one of her close friends, Karol Wojtyla, then The Archbishop of Krakow. On 16 October 1978, Karol was elected Pope John Paul II.

Afterward, Jérôme regularly travelled to Rome to meet with the Pope, to attend meetings of the Roman Catholic Church in the Academy of Sciences department to participate in other church events. The Pope wanted to name Jérôme as the president of a new Catholic Church Academy that was dear to his heart: the Church's Academy for Life. Jérôme painstakingly drafted its laws and the oath of the Servants of Life that each member of the academy must take.

Towards the end of his life, Jérôme was diagnosed with lung cancer in November 1993. He served as president of the academy for only a few weeks before his death in April 1994.

A few years later, during his visit to Paris for World Youth Day 1997, John Paul II visited Jérôme's grave in Châlo-Saint-Mars, south west of Paris. Jérôme has been named 'Servant of God' by the Catholic Church, and his cause for sainthood is being postulated by the Abbey of Saint Wandrille in France.

Legacy

What a legacy he had to find out the different chromosomes that caused Down Syndrome and many more disorders. He certainly paved the way for future doctors to find the cause of the disorders but get closer to how our genetics are made up. He certainly plays an important role in the history of disability.

Down Syndrome Today

Treating Down syndrome today comes into three categories. The first one:

Early Intervention

This provides young children with Down Syndrome a range of programs which are designed to help them gain the skills they need such as:

Feed and dress themselves.

Rolling over, crawling and then learning to walk.

Social skills around other people.

Thinking and solving problems.

Talk listen and understand others.

These programs are typically provided by teachers, therapists and physiotherapists who are experts in providing children with mental and physical support that they need.

Help in School

Every child has the right to be cared under the Individuals with Disabilities Act which is an education program that starts at the age of 3. It is to provide high quality learning based on the child's capabilities, so the curriculum isn't too hard for them but still challenging for them to learn. Additionally, it may involve working with a therapist to help with reading, writing and speech. It's very important while teaching someone with Down Syndrome to teach them at a level that they feel comfortable and to set a program that's as per their needs as each of them is unique in their special way when it comes to learning.

Medical Assistance

Children with Down Syndrome are more likely to get other illnesses:

Hearing loss-Many children with downs have headlong loss in one or both ears. This is due to the skull being shaped differently compared to normal. So, regular visits to the doctor are essential to keep them healthy. Sometimes, it's caused by fluid build-up in the ears; in this case ear tubes will be needed to not only get the fluid out of the ears but to stop ear infections.

Problems with eyesight are also common, so regular check-ups to see the doctor may be needed to look at the eyes to prescribe glasses, surgeries or other treatments to improve their sight. It's also important to keep up with eye exams, just to make sure everything is normal.

Heart problems are another concern; around half of babies who have downs have a heart problem. This is due to its shape or how the heart works. Some conditions are more serious than others which may need medication, or in wore cases, surgery to correct it.

Sleep Apnea is another condition which is linked to Down Syndrome. This is where the lungs temporarily stop while sleeping. Around the age of four, a sleep test is carried out to see how the lungs work during sleep. The main task is to see if the lungs stop and restart while sleeping. If this is the case, then a sleeping mask would be provided. The mask is attached to a machine that helps the person to breathe normally. Sometime, larger than normal tonsils and adenoids causes sleep apnea; if this is the case, then your doctor may suggest having them removed. Leukaemia is another condition that children with Down Syndrome have. But leukaemia isn't life threatening, it's a very curable condition so there's a good reason to be hopeful that things can be done to treat it. Thyroid problems are more likely to occur in those having Down syndrome. This affects people as they get older; the thyroid is located in our throat under the Adam's Apple. Our thyroids produce two hormones called thyroxine and triiodothyronine which are responsible for regulating energy levels. They also play a role in physical and mental development. The problems however start when the thyroid produces to little or too much of the hormones that can cause problems with energy levels. The symptoms to look out for when the thyroid produces little hormones (hypothyroidism) are slowing down, dry hair, weight gain, slow pulse, constipation, abnormal periods, tiredness, rough skin, hair loss, mental deterioration, deafness, anaemia. The symptoms to look out for hyperactive thyroid (Hyperthyroidism) are weight loss, increased appetite, changes in behaviour, tremors, diarrhoea, irritability, swelling of the thyroid gland, breathlessness, thinning hair, bulging eyes, palpitations. The symptoms aren't easy to spot for people with Down Syndrome but with regular check-ups, this can be done.

Today, we rely on the dedicated team of people to help patients with Down Syndrome to live a normal life. People with Down Syndrome can be capable of many dreams they put their mind to just like us. Just because they look different doesn't mean that can't dream like all of us. Just allow them to flourish in their own way and they'll get there just love them for who they are, and the rest will sort itself out.

Chapter XXIV
A Glimpse into the Future

We come to our final chapter where I give you a glimpse into what's in store for people with disability and my thoughts on the future.

Gene Editing

As time is passing by, gene editing or gene therapy as it's also known is becoming more and more popular; a procedure which involves finding the mutated gene before the baby is born or throughout life. Gene editing has been known by doctors since the 1960s but back then, there wasn't anything reliable to cut out the mutated genes accurately. In 2005, it all changed when scientists came up with a system called CRISPR CAS-9. The system works in two components-the first is the CAS-9 protein which cuts the DNA, second is the guide RNA genes which recognise the patterns of the DNA. Scientists look into the DNA patterns to find the health problem. The guide RNA follows the letter sequence ACGT which is what our DNA is made of. The guide RNA is also attached to the CAS-9 protein, so that when the RNA is searching through every letter in our DNA, it'll be able to identify the mutated gene. Then scientists have three options to edit the existing genes or to cut them out or replace them with new healthy genes. This is just a brief description on what CRISPR can do.

I have to say it does have huge potential in curing disability. However, in my opinion, there is one thing that even scientists can't control. I've talked about the other major cause of disability before which is the ever-changing environment which we don't have any control over. In my opinion, even gene editing wouldn't be able to solve this problem because even after you've edited someone's gene and the person lives in extreme hot or cold conditions, then what will happen is what happened to us approximately 200,000 years ago when we were cave men and women, our cells and our genes broke down because it couldn't keep up with the ice age.

Another problem which gene editing has: Say someone's gene has been edited and we think they are going to be fine for the rest of their life, then a different area of the genome or even the chromosome has another mutation. Gene mutations have been around with us since the start of human existence and they are highly adaptable. Just when we think that we've beaten them, they come up with another plan of being somewhere else in a different cell, gene or chromosome etc. I'm not saying that gene editing is bad, like I said it has huge potential for the future, but we have to look at the whole picture. That's one thing I love about science; there is no wrong or right way of doing things; science is full of opportunities to be looked at on how we can make our world a better place. Crisper Technology is really making its existence. In the near future, because of changes taking place in science, disability will also change and probably be cured. There are seven diseases that could be cured with gene editing:

Cancer.

Blood condition.

Blindness.

AIDS.

Cystic Fibrosis.

Muscular Dystrophy.

Huntington's Disease.

Cancer

Gene editing could one day be the forefront of curing cancer. It works by taking the T-Cells from the cancer patient which are vital for attacking the cancer cells. Crisper comes along and finds the gene mutation which causes the cancer cells to be visible and thrive. They then bind together a protein called PD-1 which is responsible for regulating the immune response throughout the human body. After crisper has taken out the T-Cells, they are modified to be stronger and out back into the body so that they defeat the cancer cells. It's still early days but it's very promising news. The earliest trials are currently being done in China where they are testing out the gene editing tools to try to treat an advanced form of cancer in the oesophagus (a long tube which connects our throats to our stomachs); at least 86 people are being trialled, in America, they have only just started in testing out their first few patients. In the University of Pennsylvania, they are removing the PD-1 protein to change the molecule on the surface of the immune to find and attack the tumours.

Blood Disorders

The first testing started in some countries in Europe and in America, scientists stared using Crisper in early February 2019. The blood disorders that they were being tested were sickles disease and beta-thalassemia which are both related to oxygen travelling around the body in the blood stream. The idea was to harvest bone marrow stem cells from the patient and using crisper technology to produce foetal haemoglobin (Natural form of oxygen carrying protein) that binds oxygen much better than the adult form. Haemophilia is another blood disorder which gene editing could cure in the future.

Blindness

Crisper would be the ideal candidate to cure blindness as there are many gene mutations which cause blindness; crisper technology would be able to search for the mutated gene and take it out and replace it with a better version of the gene, then it will be placed back into our DNA.

The downside to gene editing at the moment is that it's going to cost a lot of money because gene editing can only treat one gene at a time. The rarer the gene mutation, the more expensive it is going to be to treat. Plus, gene editing isn't good for everyone because gene editing has a different response from different people. But there is a glimpse of hope as of now as bigger companies are merging together to come up with the funds to pay more for research of gene mutations to allow this treatment to advance so that gene editing will become suitable for everyone. If we take retinitis pigmentosa which causes blindness, for example, one day it will be advanced enough to help 60 different gene mutations that causes retinitis pigmentosa. Crisper is by no means the only thing that will cure blindness. There is always science and technology that are getting better every day. For example, bionic eyes, which works by inserting a chip in the eyes, is a grid of electrodes that stimulate the retina receptors at the back of the eye. Then flashes of light appear in the retina which allows the patient to see. The vision isn't quite the same as a person with normal vision, but it allows people to see in a grid format which is a huge leap forward. A massive step in treating retinitis pigmentosa, bionic eyes do need more time to improve.

AIDS

Gene editing could be the future for curing AIDS. This research is only in its infancy but scientists are getting closer as we speak. They do this with the crisper technology to remove the mutated gene and replace it with a healthy version of the gene or cut it out permanently to cure the patient of AIDS. So far tests for this have only been done on lab rats. These rats had AIDS and were injected with a harmless virus which makes a version of the crisper enzyme technology which destroys the HIV genes which hide in the mice's DNA. It's in really early stages at the moment as gene editing is only cutting and replacing the genes in the DNA. In order for this to be a cure, we need to destroy the HIV cells which are not only located in our genes, but they can also appear as cells which hover throughout our bodies, including in the bone marrow, brain, and lymph nodes etc. Crisper technology isn't advanced enough to tackle this at the moment but at least we know where the HIV virus is, and we just need more research to make it stronger and, in the future, it'll be a very reliable way to cure aids.

Cystic Fibrosis

Gene editing could one day be able to treat Cystic Fibrosis by using Crisper technology which is used to locate the mutated gene (CFTR). The most challenging part in the gene editing process is to get into the patient's cell nucleus but once inside, the crisper technology will be able to find the mutated gene and cut it of the DNA and replace it with a new and healthy gene. One of the positive things about gene editing is that once the new and healthy gene is in place, it is permanent, so the patient wouldn't need any more treatment. The challenges that it faces are that it can only correct one mutation at a time where for CF mutation there are about 1,700 different mutations which cause Cystic Fibrosis. Researchers are currently advancing or finding other ways to treat more or all of the mutations. The future certainly looks bright for people suffering with CF.

Muscular Dystrophy

Gene editing could also be at the for front of tackling muscular dystrophy for good as researchers are exploring the possibilities of what gene editing could eventually do for patients with MD. Researchers began by extracting muscle cells that have MD and brought them into the lab to use Crisper technology. After a few years of trial and error, they finally made a breakthrough in restoring the production in dystrophin which is the protein that maintains the strength of muscles. In order to make sure they had found the solution, they reimplanted the muscle tissue into mice, they found that the mice were capable of making human dystrophin protein. This allowed the Crisper/Cas9 system to find the mutated dystrophin gene, cut it out and replace it with a healthy dystrophin gene. The healthier gene will be a shorter version, but it'll still be able to function normally. However, the shorter gene doesn't mean that it'll cure them, but it'll help the symptoms improve into Becker muscular dystrophy which is a milder version of muscular dystrophy. If it's proved successful, then we could see a 45–55% increase in treating patients with MD which is huge from nothing at all; there are roughly 2,500 people living with MD in the UK right now and there aren't any efficient treatments or cures.

Huntington's Disease

For Huntington's Disease, this revolutionary technology would be able to cure the disease just like the other conditions by cutting out the gene and replacing it with a healthy HTT gene. The research is still in its infancy just like the rest of the other diseases, but progress has been made on successfully trialling it on human samples of DNA. The only concern that we have right now is that what the long-term effects of gene editing are? What the side effects are? We do know that this is permanent treatment that could last a lifetime which is a truly ground-breaking thought in medicine. We haven't had a breakthrough like this since the discovery of these diseases. One day, we won't have them anymore as gene editing has changed human history forever.

My concerns for gene editing is not the side effects, but how would gene editing adapt to our ever-changing environment and extreme weather. Could it save our genes through an ice age or a heat wave? Could gene editing save our genetics if we get enough nutrients in the body? Will gene editing in the future create an unfair advantage against people who have had their genes edited in our society? Other than that, I will look forward to seeing what gene editing will have to offer us all. Maybe one day disability will be nothing but a distant memory.

The End

Well, here we are we have reached the end of the story. We've travelled back to 250,000 years' worth of human history. A secret human history which has allowed us to travel Europe and America and give a brief look into Asia. I hope I've helped in expanding your knowledge in disability. What we can take from this is knowing that disability is not a curse that our ancestors thought we had. Those thoughts of curses only came from fear which is why I kept repeating in the book that the only thing that could've saved our genetics was evolution. But we didn't have the right amount of nutrients to keep genetics healthy. Disability even starts before the growing process in the womb; it's just after the fertilisation of an egg, the Big Bang of X-Cells explodes and attack the good cells but the good cells also attack the bad, which is why disability is a lottery.

Disability makes our bodies look different. I hope that with this newfound knowledge, you will help people have the confidence to say hi to a disabled person in public and treat them like a normal human being. As I've explained, disabled people have a unique history just like able-bodied people do. I know it's easy to judge someone by their appearance, but you never know they could be the smartest, the funniest, the most caring people you'll ever meet even if they are in a wheelchair. Disability teaches us that not one of us is the same; we are all different. It teaches us to adapt and change to survive. The most important lesson that disability teaches us is that we are all defined by our minds not our bodies as we are all spiritual beings encased in a human body.

Thank you for reading this adventure, I hope this is a start of a true deep understanding of disabled people as a whole rather than looking at them through stigma.

References

1. The X-Cell Theory comes from my own notes
2. Disability in the Middle Ages-
    https://mn.gov/mnddc/parallels/two/1.html
3. Disability in England-
    https://historicengland.org.uk/research/inclusive-heritage/disability-history/1050-1485/
4. The Founding Fathers of Disability—
    https://www.livescience.com/62515-hippocrates.html
    (Hippocrates) (Galen)
5. *https://www.ucl.ac.uk/~ucgajpd/medicina%20antiqua/bio_gal.html*
6. The history of Cerebral Palsy-
    https://www.thecerebralpalsysite.co.uk/origin-history-cerebral-palsy/
7. William John Little-
    https://www.ncbi.nlm.nih.gov/pmc/articles/PMC4859855/
8. Sigmund Freud-*https://en.wikipedia.org/wiki/Sigmund_Freud*
9. Part 2 of Sigmund's life
    https://www.biography.com/scholar/sigmund-freud
10. William Osler—
    https://medicalarchives.jhmi.edu:8443/osler/biography.htm
11. The History of Dwarfism-*https://wsedwarfism.weebly.com/the-history-of-dwarfism.html*
12. The History of Osteogenesis Imperfecta-
    https://www.ncbi.nlm.nih.gov/pmc/articles/PMC516444/Skeletal Dysplasia-https://www.ncbi.nlm.nih.gov/pubmed/19006207
13. Jean Lobstein-*https://en.wikipedia.org/wiki/Jean_Lobstein*
14. Willem Vrolik-*https://en.wikipedia.org/wiki/Willem_Vrolik*

15. Genetics of Osteogenesis Imperfecta—
    https://ghr.nlm.nih.gov/condition/osteogenesis-imperfecta
16. The history of Motor Neurone Disease-*https://rcni.com/hosted-content/rcn/mnd/what-motor-neurone-disease*
17. Jean Martin Charcot-*https://en.wikipedia.org/wiki/Jean-Martin_Charcot*
18. The History of Polio-
    https://amhistory.si.edu/polio/timeline/index.htm
19. Franklin D. Roosevelt and Polio-*https://www.fdrlibrary.org/polio*
20. The life of Karl Landsteiner (co-founder of poliomyelitis)—
    https://www.nobelprize.org/prizes/medicine/1930/landsteiner/biographical/
21. The History of Meningitis-*https://www.news-medical.net/health/History-of-Meningitis.aspx*
22. The life of Sir Robert Whytt-
    https://www.rcpe.ac.uk/heritage/college-history/robert-whytt
23. The genetics of meningitis-
    https://www.theguardian.com/lifeandstyle/2010/aug/09/meningitis-linked-gene-mutations
24. The History of Paralysis-*https://pmj.bmj.com/content/81/952/108*
25. The definition of Paralysis-
    https://www.healthline.com/health/paralysis
26. Sir Charles Bell—*https://en.wikipedia.org/wiki/Charles_Bell*
27. The Genetics of Paralysis-
    https://ghr.nlm.nih.gov/condition/infantile-onset-ascending-hereditary-spastic-paralysis#genes
28. The History of Epilepsy—
    https://www.hindawi.com/journals/ert/2014/582039/
29. John Hughlings Jackson (father of Epilepsy)-
    https://en.wikipedia.org/wiki/John_Hughlings_Jackson
30. The History of Epilepsy Medicine-
    https://www.hindawi.com/journals/ert/2014/582039/

31. The History of Multiple Sclerosis-*https://mymsaa.org/ms-information/overview/history/*

32. Definition of Multiple Sclerosis-*https://www.mssociety.org.uk/about-ms/what-is-ms Genetics of Multiple Sclerosis—https://www.nationalmssociety.org/What-is-MS/What-Causes-MS*

33. The History of Cystic Fibrosis—*https://www.nationaljewish.org/conditions/cystic-fibrosis-cf/history*

34. Life of Dorothy Hansine Anderson—*https://cfmedicine.nlm.nih.gov/physicians/biography_8.html*

35. Life of Paul Di Sant Agnese-*https://www.cff.org/Research/Researcher-Resources/North-American-CF-Conference/Paul-di-Sant-Agnese-Distinguished-Scientific-Achievement-Award/*

36. Genetics of Cystic Fibrosis-*https://ghr.nlm.nih.gov/condition/cystic-fibrosis*

37. The History of Spina Bifida-Original Source (Deleted) so a second reference *https://adc.bmj.com/content/archdischild/39/203/41.full.pdf*

38. What Spina Bifida is-*https://www.shinecharity.org.uk/spina-bifida/what-is-spina-bifida*

39. The life of Rudolf Virchow-*https://www.famousscientists.org/rudolf-virchow/*

40. The life of James Morton—*https://www.theglasgowstory.com/image/?inum=TGSJ00045*

41. The History of Muscular Dystrophy—*https://www.researchgate.net/publication/300176024_Muscular_Dystrophy_Historical_Background_and_Types*

42. What is Muscular Dystrophy-*https://www.genome.gov/Genetic-Disorders/Duchenne-Muscular-Dystrophy*

43. The genetics of muscular dystrophy—*https://ghr.nlm.nih.gov/gene/DMD#normalfunction*

44. The life of Guillaume-Benjamin-Amand Duchenne—
    https://en.m.wikipedia.org/wiki/Duchenne_de_Boulogne

45. The History of Tourette's syndrome—
    https://en.m.wikipedia.org/wiki/History_of_Tourette_syndrome

46. The life of Georges Gilles de la Tourette—*https://tourette.ca/the-man-behind-the-name-gilles-de-la-tourettes-story/*

47. The life of Arthur K Shapiro—
    https://en.wikipedia.org/wiki/Arthur_K._Shapiro

48. The History of The Deaf—*https://www.historytoday.com/no-longer-deaf-past*

49. The History of Deaf Education Part 1—
    https://www.bslzone.co.uk/watch/history-deaf-education-1/

50. The History of Deaf people Part 2—
    https://www.bslzone.co.uk/watch/history-deaf-education-2/

51. The life of John Bulwer—
    https://en.m.wikipedia.org/wiki/John_Bulwer

52. The life of Thomas Braidwood—
    https://en.wikipedia.org/wiki/Thomas_Braidwood

53. The Life of Charles-Michel de l'Épée—
    https://en.m.wikipedia.org/wiki/Charles-Michel_de_l%27Épée

54. The life of Samuel Heinicke—
    https://www.verywellhealth.com/samuel-heinicke-oral-education-1046549

55. The life of Laurent Clerc—
    https://en.wikipedia.org/wiki/Laurent_Clerc

56. The life of Ray Kay Holcomb—
    http://deafpeople.com/history/history_info/roy_holcomb.html

57. Part 2 *https://prezi.com/p/swlxphha8ouk/asl-roy-kay-holcomb-project/*

58. The life of Alice Cogswell-*https://www.startasl.com/alice-cogswell/*

59. The Genetics of Deafness-*https://ghr.nlm.nih.gov/gene/GJB2*

60. The life of Beethoven-
    https://www.biography.com/musician/ludwig-van-beethoven
61. The life of Hellen Keller-
    https://www.biography.com/activist/helen-keller
62. The History of Blindness-
    https://www.britannica.com/topic/history-of-the-blind-1996241
63. The life of Louis Braille-*https://www.royalblind.org/national-braille-week/about-braille/who-was-louis-braille*
64. The life of Edward Rushton—*https://www.bbc.co.uk/news/blogs-ouch-29957645*
65. Causes of Blindness—
    https://www.medicinenet.com/blindness/article.htm
66. Blindness Education history in America—
    https://www3.gallaudet.edu/clerc-center/info-to-go/deaf-education/200-years-of-deaf-education.html
67. Genetics of Blindness—
    https://my.clevelandclinic.org/health/diseases/17130-inherited-eye-disease
68. The History of Huntington's Disease—
    https://www.huntingtonsnsw.org.au/information/hd-facts/history
69. The life of George Huntington—
    https://link.springer.com/article/10.1007/s00415-018-8860-5
70. The Genetics of Huntington's Disease—
    https://ghr.nlm.nih.gov/condition/huntington-disease
71. The History of Locked in Syndrome—
    https://www.ncbi.nlm.nih.gov/pmc/articles/PMC549115/
72. The life of Fred Plum—
    https://www.nytimes.com/2010/06/13/health/13plum.html?mtrref=undefined&gwh=F4F8D8887043EF94CD7C2BEB9D1AEA86&gwt=pay&assetType=REGIWALL
73. Treating locked in Syndrome—
    https://rarediseases.info.nih.gov/diseases/6919/locked-in-syndrome

74. The Glasgow Coma Scale—
    https://en.wikipedia.org/wiki/Glasgow_Coma_Scale

75. The History of Scoliosis—
    https://www.ncbi.nlm.nih.gov/pmc/articles/PMC3566253/

76. Thoracolumbar Scoliosis—
    https://www.scoliosissos.com/news/post/thoracolumbar-scoliosis-explained

77. Lumbar Scoliosis-
    https://www.scoliosissos.com/news/post/lumbar-scoliosis-treatment

78. Kyphosis Scoliosis-*https://orthoinfo.aaos.org/en/diseases--conditions/kyphosis-roundback-of-the-spine/*

79. King Tutankhamun and Scoliosis—
    https://www.hudsonvalleyscoliosis.com/king-tutankhamun-scoliosis/

80. Ambroise Paire and his Iron Corsets—
    https://www.ncbi.nlm.nih.gov/pmc/articles/PMC1079595/

81. The discovery of X-Rays-*https://www.nde-ed.org/EducationResources/HighSchool/Radiography/discoveryxrays.htm*

82. The life of Wilhelm Conrad Röntgen—
    https://www.nobelprize.org/prizes/physics/1901/rontgen/biographical/

83. The genetics of scoliosis-
    https://www.treatingscoliosis.com/blog/is-scoliosis-hereditary-genetic-environmental/

84. The History of Parkinson's Disease—
    https://en.wikipedia.org/wiki/History_of_Parkinson%27s_disease

85. The symptoms of Parkinson's—
    https://www.mayoclinic.org/diseases-conditions/parkinsons-disease/symptoms-causes/syc-20376055

86. The Rates of getting Parkinson's Disease-*https://parkinsonsnewstoday.com/parkinsons-disease-statistics/*

87. The life of James Parkinson-*https://www.sunsigns.org/famousbirthdays/profile/james-parkinson/*

88. The Genetics of Parkinson's-*https://ghr.nlm.nih.gov/gene/SNCA*

89. The History of Down Syndrome-*https://www.nads.org/about-us/history-of-nads/*

90. The symptoms of Down's Syndrome-*https://www.nads.org/about-us/history-of-nads/*

91. The life of John Langdon-*https://touchdown21.info/en/page/5-trisomy-21/article/200-who-was-john-langdon-down.html*

92. The life of Jérôme Lejeune-*http://www.ncregister.com/blog/pattyknap/dr.-jerome-lejeune-hero-of-the-pro-life-movement*

93. Cru Cat Syndrome-*https://www.genome.gov/Genetic-Disorders/Cri-du-Chat*

94. Earliest case of Down syndrome ever found—*https://www.livescience.com/46721-earliest-down-syndrome-skeleton-discovered.html*

95. Gene editing—*https://ghr.nlm.nih.gov/primer/genomicresearch/genomeediting*

96. 7 Disabilities that gene editing could one day cure-*https://www.labiotech.eu/tops/crispr-technology-cure-disease/*

Milton Keynes UK
Ingram Content Group UK Ltd.
UKHW022032181123
432826UK00004B/61

9 781035 826674